INVITATION TO DISCIPLESHIP

ADULT INQUIRER'S MANUAL
BY MARTIN E. MARTY

AUGSBURG PUBLISHING HOUSE
MINNEAPOLIS

INVITATION TO DISCIPLESHIP
Adult Inquirer's Manual

Prepared under the auspices of the Division for Life and Mission in the Congregation and the Board of Publication of the American Lutheran Church

This Inquirer's Manual is accompanied by a Leader Guide

Gloria E. Bengtson, Kristine L. M. Carlson, and Ann Harrington, editors
Koechel/Peterson Design, design

Photos: Dale R. Peterson, 4; Mark Gonnerman, 9; Barry Henderson, 14, 21; Michael Burkey, 18; Religious News Service, 26, 44, 76; Religious News Service by Robert Klein, 52; Roger W. Neal, 29; Deborah Gorman, 32, 85; Katherine Heister, 35; Mimi Forsyth, 39; Edward Wallowitch, 48, 56; John J. Swartz, 61; Stewart M. Green, 64; Jean-Claude Lejeune, 69; Christopher Postel, 73; Jonathan A. Meyers, 80; Dale D. Gehman, 88; John Meaney, 90; Ron Meyer, 94; Robert Hill, 97; Paul M. Schrock, 100; H. Armstrong Roberts, 107.

Scripture quotations unless otherwise noted are from Revised Standard Version of the Bible, copyright 1946-71 by Division of Christian Education, National Council of Churches, and are used by permission.

Excerpts from the New Jerusalem Bible copyright © 1985 by Darton, Longman & Todd, Ltd. and Doubleday & Company, Inc. reprinted by permission of the publisher.

Catechism quotations are from *The Small Catechism by Martin Luther in Contemporary English with Lutheran Book of Worship Texts*, copyright 1968 by Augsburg Publishing House, the Board of Publication of the Lutheran Church in America, and Concordia Publishing House; used by permission.

Materials identified as *LBW* are reprinted from *Lutheran Book of Worship*, copyright © 1978.

Manufactured in U.S.A.

2   3   4   5   6   7   8   9   0   1   2   3   4   5   6   7   8   9

Contents

1
An Inviting Church

THE CRITICAL QUESTION

Do I belong here?

You have asked that question before. You've been invited to a party. Will you feel comfortable there? The members of an old club have gathered; they all know each other. Will they accept you? A class is forming. Are the others too smart, or too advanced for you? Are you "out of your class"?

Do I belong here? That is a natural question when people gather who are inquiring about a faith and about a church. We often ask the question about belonging with a bit of fear. We may be uneasy. It's a bit frightening.

Everything new is frightening. When what is new has to do with urgent issues, newness can be even scarier. Inquirers wondering about their health may tremble at the clinic. Those examining their financial condition may do so with a racing pulse. And now, as we begin to take up matters that affect the deepest, most intimate—yes, we may even say *eternal*—issues, we have reason to be a bit uneasy at first.

If you could visit groups of inquirers all over the map and everywhere in the church, you might find that a typical group would include uneasy people like these:

Two people have fallen in love and are to be married. One is a Lutheran. The other is not; he or she may be of another Christian church body or may not have been brought up in the faith. "Your church or mine?" such couples often ask. Some answer, "Both." Some answer, "Neither." Many want to inquire. They want to see whether they can share a way to express the love of God while they deepen their love for each other. They have many things to be joyful about, with their life of love ahead of them. Yet they are a bit frightened about all the choices and demands. Inquiring about faith is one more thing to be worked out.

Do I belong here? is also the question of others who came almost casually. Maybe she found this church in the Yellow Pages, or he came because of a news story or an advertisement in Saturday's newspaper. It could be that a college course on religion inspired questions for another. Coming to an adult inquirer's class at church, people wonder, Is this the place to have the questions addressed? The answer is yes.

Do I belong here? A retired person may have volunteered for activities to help others, and in this way come into contact with church members, who then invited him to join with them in worship. A young couple wants to pass on the faith to their two small children, but they want to know what it is to pass on the faith, and what the faith is to pass on. They want to stay ahead of their children's questions, and they have some of their own.

Do I belong here? That's a natural question for someone who is church-shopping. Have you ever been in a department store, wanting to take a quick peek at the merchandise and price tags, only to be nabbed by a pushy sales clerk who won't let you go? Perhaps you wonder, could this church be that way too? If I show interest, can I ever back off? Can I just quietly disappear and not be pestered? If not, should I back off now before people know my name?

We mention all these ways to feel unsettled or scared because the feeling comes to most people. The question of belonging is a natural one. How do we answer it? One way might be to say, "There's nothing to worry about. You're among friends. It's easy." Another might suggest, "Let's make the most of our slight case of nerves. People often learn best when they are on edge. Ask the athletes, or people who have to take examinations. It's good to feel edgy. We are going to be talking about life-and-death matters, and you should not take them casually."

We are going to talk about God. That's a short syllable. Everyone uses the word. Some use it for profanity. Others gasp it in prayer. A few seem to know all about what it means. Perhaps we have some sense of fear or awe when we speak of God. In the Bible we hear of people who take the shoes off their feet when they are in the presence of God. They shudder when God is vivid in the temple. If God is More than all that we can know, if God is Other in ways that we do not understand, it is good to feel off balance a bit as we inquire.

Do I belong here? Though it may kill some suspense, the answer has to be yes. Whether people come to classes like this by twos or tens, by accident, or because a friend or relative urged them, they come to know that the real inviter is God. And God is one who accepts us even when no one else does—even when we cannot accept ourselves. God invites anybody and everybody and says, "Make yourselves at home. This is my house. These are my people. I want to reach you all with my love." God may be all-powerful, but this God does not force you to stay against your will. Neither do the people who speak in God's name. Yet the love of God often reaches us through people—people who make up classes, or start churches, or guide inquirers. And they, too, try to say, "You belong" in this inviting church. The best way to test ourselves, our inviters, and our God is to do the inquiring. Let's begin together.

THE PRESENTATION

Let's use a church building as a model for inquiring. A class of adult inquirers may not be meeting in a *sanctuary,* that is, a room for divine worship. Such a group may meet instead in an education room, a church hall, a school, a home, or under a summer's sky, for that matter. Yet it is not likely that many who explore a faith have never been inside a place where its believers worship. We can use images of such a place as a model of what follows.

Think of the place of local worship as a kind of port of entry for the whole faith, for the whole church. Whatever you will need in order to understand Lutheran Christianity you can get locally, in that room and in what that room stands for. You do not have to make a pilgrimage to the Holy Land, nor must you get a visa to East Germany to see where Martin Luther lived and taught five centuries ago. You can go through life in your local church and never visit the national offices of your denomination or even know where they are, though you would be welcome there. Local Christians are part of the whole Christian church. They connect with Lutherans and other Christians everywhere. Yet you can stay home, right here, and gain access to it all.

So we are at a port of entry, where newcomers look things over. Let's enter and look around.

If this is an inviting church, it has to invite. A sign outside probably says "Everyone Welcome" or "All Are Invited." The people who put that sign there speak in the name of God who is the all-welcoming inviter. This God is their model. And so they open the door—perhaps a big door, perhaps one painted red so you cannot miss it. It is an image of welcome.

A *font*. One of the first things you will see is a place for baptizing. Some churches have it near the entrance, to suggest that this is how we are received by God. Others keep it up front, where the congregation can see the Baptisms. A font may be a little stand with a basin, or a sculptured rock. In a Lutheran church it is not likely to be a small pool, as it would be in a Baptist church or some other churches. Whatever its placement or size, it has to hold water, the earthly element in this washing of sins and for this initiation into God's family.

If you have witnessed a font in use at a Baptism, whether of a child or an adult. you heard words like these: "We are born children of a fallen humanity; in the waters of Baptism we are reborn children of God and inheritors of eternal life. By water and the Holy Spirit we are made members of the Church which is the body of Christ. As we live with him and with his people, we grow in faith, love, and obedience to the will of God."

Maybe one phrase caught your ear: "we are reborn," and you thought, so Lutherans and others who baptize this way belong to the "born-again" movement. You may not have known that, because Lutherans do not always use such language when they greet you or ask about your relation to God. Yet that font and its water remind us that we have to be "born from above," "born again," or "reborn," and that Baptism is the great sign of our rebirth. Lutherans are so "born again"-minded that they want you to hear the word of God every day, the word that asks you to repent, turn away from your old self, old ways, old sins, and let God give you love and grace. You will be asked to be born again and again and again, daily. The invitation to such a rich experience helps make this an inviting church. And the font reminds us of our rebirth.

Do I belong here? Is this an inviting church? The second piece of furniture in this place of worship helps give an answer. It is an *altar* or a table. If the font was off center, this object is likely to be

in the center. Lutherans have no magical view of their altar or table. They can commune with their Lord without one. If you are in an intensive-care unit at a hospital, they will bring you the little trace of bread and wine that the physicians allow, and you may feel more than ever that you are at the Lord's banquet. What's more, their military chaplains have used even the hoods of jeeps or a fallen tree to hold the bread and wine and book. Yet when Lutherans can settle down in a house of God, they place the same importance on the altar or table for their Christian life as they do on their kitchen or dining room table to life at home.

In ancient days, as in the Hebrew Scriptures, the altar was used to sacrifice animals or to bring gifts of grain and grape. Christians today, Lutherans among them, tell stories of those ancient days. They let an altar serve as an image for the way Jesus Christ was offered as a sacrifice for them. Such language is often hard to grasp, but most Christians sense in their hearts what their mind does not always catch at once or in detail. Indeed, Christians know that the story will always remain partly mysterious. It is the sense or knowledge that when Jesus gave up his life, when his blood was shed, he was their innocent representative. Hate, injustice, power, sin—all these took their toll. The world has no room for his perfect love. It tries to get rid of him, it puts him to death. The altar is a reminder of the sacrifice.

Yet the altar is also a table for a meal. What better way to test an inviting church than to be welcomed at a meal! Sharing a meal is a special part of life. Young lovers court at romantic restaurants. We raise funds, honor heroes and heroines, make up our minds about politics, and entertain friends at a table. Lutheran Christians like to gather at this table. They don't call it "The Lutheran table" or "First Church's table." It is the Lord's table for the Lord's Supper. The table is a reminder of the last meal Jesus ate with his friends and disciples before he died. At this last meal Jesus told his disciples to eat bread and drink wine in the days to come. He said he would be there with them when they did. He also said he wanted to eat this meal with them in a heavenly banquet. And he will. Meanwhile, it is this Lord who welcomes Christian believers regularly. They are "born children of a fallen humanity," and they fall into sin regularly. But when the ministers hand out the bread and wine in and with which Jesus is present, they are saying, in effect, "Take it, it's for sinners."

So there's a font for initiation and a table for nurture. Now your eye falls on a third piece of furniture. It may be a *pulpit,* a *lectern,* a reading stand, a place to hold a book. In some churches the minister simply stands near the altar to speak. Most of the time, though, this bookstand is rather prominent, sometimes raised and usually well-lighted. Such accents are there to suggest that something important goes on here. This is a place for speaking, for encouraging, for judging, for offering the activity of God. The Lutherans, the Bible, and most other Christians call this *preaching,* and make much of it.

If you stayed to hear a preacher, you learned again why this is an inviting church. Preachers prepare for their message. They use memorable stories and images if they can. They strive for some eloquence and passion, even if their words are not flowery and they do not raise their voices. Why? Because they are speaking the word of God in each gathering.

They use language for inquirers, like the word of the Lord in Jeremiah 29:13-14: "You will seek me and find me; when you seek me with all your heart, I will be found by you, says the Lord." They use language for those who have been invited, like the word of the

Lord in Matthew 11:28: "Come to me, all who labor and are heavy laden, and I will give you rest. Take my yoke upon you, and learn from me; for I am gentle and lowly in heart, and you will find rest for your souls." They will tell stories like the one in Luke 14:23 that ends with the master saying to a servant, "Go out to the highways and hedges. and compel people to come in, that my house may be filled." They are talking about God and talking for God, who invites people who expect no invitation, who invites people to take the places of those who turned their backs. Lutherans believe that even though the speaker is also a fallen sinner, even though the grammar may not always be perfect and even though there can be a lisp of speech or a lapse in thought, God's word is being spoken here.

The font is used once per life. The table is used frequently, perhaps weekly, for the Lord's Supper and whenever Christians gather to offer prayer to God. The pulpit may be pounded and its podium worn from constant use. Picture the three together—font, table, and pulpit—as poles around which Lutheran worship revolves. Yet there is a fourth place in a sanctuary that is important: the *pews* or chairs where the congregation sits, stands, and perhaps kneels in worship.

The *congregation*. Those who are "born children of a fallen humanity." Like you. These are people who are not perfect. In case you think they are, or in case you think they think they are, stick around and get to know them. They can be weak and petty and mean. They are here because they know they can be weak and petty and mean, and often are. They have simply accepted an invitation and are equipping themselves to extend more invitations. They are like hungry people who know where to find food. Here, in this inviting church. In case you think these imperfect people are not capable of being changed, of responding to God's invitation, stick around and get to know them. Recall the words quoted earlier from the Service of Holy Baptism: as "reborn children of God" they are to "live with him and with his people," to "grow in faith, love, and obedience to the will of God." They are to be "in Christ," or "like Christ," when God looks upon them as reborn children—God's own. They often overcome their old selves and let the new life in Christ show. They can then be generous and sacrificial. In such congregations you will feel the support of prayer and the works of love.

THE STUDY

As members of the congregation are gathered in a place of worship, one might wonder, Do *they* belong here? They do, because they have the one needed and proper credential: a desire to praise God. If we study them in the act of praising, we will begin to learn what Lutherans think Christian worship and life are about.

A wise Lutheran named Joseph Sittler once reminded his fellow believers that when they praise God they are doing something the church alone is equipped to do. Anyone, he says, can have duplicating and mailing machines, heat and light bills, committees and task forces, agencies for doing good. But the church exists to return thanks to God. The church exists to remind the world of the source of its life and its good. When Martin Luther preached a sermon dedicating the first chapel built for Protestant worship, he came to the point: Nothing, he said, should ever happen there except that our dear Lord speaks to us through his holy word, and we in turn respond in prayer and praise.

What good does that do? Lutherans would answer that there is a prior point. Before they get practical about worship, they will tell you that it should reflect How Things Are. In their reading of the Bible, How Things Are goes something like this: the God they worship created and creates the world, out of a desire for relationship. God makes humans in the divine image, makes a world, calls it good, gives it life. This God reaches into the world of a fallen humanity in Jesus Christ, out of a need to restore a relationship. God does this simply out of divine love. That is how things are. When believers worship and praise, when they lift up hands in prayer or voices in song, they are making a statement about the universe. They do not picture God as one who has to be constantly admired. They do picture that in worship they are reordering their lives, they are helping set the world right. Whenever they praise God they are recognizing God as the source of life; they are learning how to care for the world and its people.

Lutheran worship, then, is God-centered. It is *theocentric (theo* is the Greek word for God). It is not human-centered, or *anthropocentric (anthropos* is the Greek word for "human"). Of course, God cares about humans; enough to have made them and to have sent Jesus Christ to keep them. Of course, human experience and emotion are important. But as you hear the Lutheran hymns you may note a consistent strain. They don't keep telling God how the believers feel at the moment—except as invited people who are now praising God. God, not human emotions, is the subject of the prayers and hymns. Lutheran worshipers believe that things go best for humans when they are on course with God and God's ways. They are less interested in philosophies of positive thinking or techniques for earthly success than in returning praise and thanks to their loving God.

Someone once wrote a book about Luther's thought. He called it *Let God Be God*. Lutherans at worship believe they are letting God be God in their praise. When God is God, then everyone is welcome, and the church is not a club. When God is God, sinners are welcome, and the church is not a society of achievers. When God is God, inquirers are treated with respect, for God does not force anything on anyone. When God is God, the church is inviting: it sends out invitations in God's name and does what it can to make its worship and ways inviting.

To study the Christian life as Lutherans picture it, we may use books, including this manual for inquirers. Yet observing this congregation in worship remains like the port of entry, a place to get an idea of what the books are out to say. If you are inquiring, you may wonder what else is required of you. Clubs have rules, societies have standards, even churches have constitutions. You know that some religions have long lists of dos and don'ts, of commands and requirements. It is very satisfying to have these lists. With such a scorecard it is easy to measure growth. One can tell where the boundaries are between those who belong and everybody else. It is frustrating that Lutherans don't hand you such a list.

Study the Lutherans as they baptize and grow in obedience to the will of God, or as they share the Lord's table, or hear the word of God. What is expected of them? Maybe we can get a clue from the offering.

The *offering*. Do I belong here? Is the church interested in me for my money, as little as I may have? People will bring up the subject of money to support institutions sooner or later. Better sooner than later. Better openly than sneakily. What's involved?

Lutheran Book of Worship directs, "The offering is received as the Lord's table is prepared." Then people sing not about money, but about vineyards and harvest and seeds and bread and prayers as offering. And there may be a prayer that says "we offer with joy and thanksgiving what you have first given us—our selves, our time, and our possessions, signs of your gracious love." Or "we offer ourselves" with "these gifts."

We offer ourselves. That's the point of it all. The money we give may help heat the place of worship, or pay for the Sunday bulletin or for a doctor in New Guinea or a New Testament professor. We offer to make that possible. What is at stake, though, is the offering of ourselves. Jesus said, "For where your treasure is, there will your heart be also" (Matthew 6:21). The worshipers are

not to step back and take a look at life and then open their pocketbooks. They are to toss their possessions on this moving train—and then keep up with it. They will soon learn that if they toss their selves on it, they will find their hearts located at a new place: in the loving purposes of God.

Study these worshipers and what they say they are about now. They have offered themselves; they are to "grow in obedience." Their hearts are now with God and the ways of God that they have praised. If so, we should follow them out the door as they disperse. Some of them have children in hand, children who have worshiped with them or who have been worshiping and learning in church school. Walking hand in hand is a symbol of the message of God's love and the activity of praise and obedience being transmitted across generations.

These people, as often single as married or in a family, disperse into communities, to distant farms and nearby high-rises. They may come together for church activities during the week, but for most of the next 167 hours they will be out in the world. There may be 400 worshipers, 100 families, 20 meetings, 2 services of worship. But there will now be, among them, a week's worth of temptations by the millions and opportunities by the millions. Most places that the church can go only the laity can go. They outnumber ministers 400 to one. No, they *are* ministers, in different places. Study them as they go to their homes and parties, their offices and factories and farms, their unemployment offices or sickrooms.

If they offered themselves, they give each day back to God. Many may make the sign of the cross at the start of the day; you won't see this, because it is part of their praise in private. This is the way they remember their Baptism. It's not a magic act, but a reminder. They are free for the day. They have no guilt about yesterday, no worry about tomorrow. God will give strength and grace for the day.

Many will now be good stewards. We do not use that word much, but in the Bible it appears often. The steward is trusted to take care of property and business for someone else. Lutheran Christians make a great deal of the way they are to be stewards of creation. They are not to misuse resources. They are to be stewards of human relations. Their faith is measured not by how many nights a week they will return to keep the church lights on. It is measured by how they relate to parents or children, how they serve on hospital or zoning or school boards, how they transact business. They get to turn each day back to God that way. If they succeed they will not become prideful, and if they fail they will not despair. Theirs is a theocentric, God-centered faith. They trust.

Stewardship means filling out the church's calendar of doings and dealings. Some will rehearse in a choir, to offer praise in beautiful song. Others will make layettes for Lutheran World Relief or visit the sick, attend committee meetings or serve as trustees of church property. What is not on the calendar is just as important and revealing. The ways of obedience and love are as varied as the persons seeking to obey and love. You belong if you can turn back your person and your ways to God. In doing so, you get to show forth the person and the ways of Christ in the world.

SUMMARY AND REFLECTION

One more thing remains to be said. We asked, Do I belong here? and addressed it to a class of inquirers at a Lutheran church. This is not the only "here," and we would do well to look beyond the circle of two or twenty at this place. Do Lutherans think this is the only "here"? An encyclopedia tells us the astounding fact that there are over 20,000 separate Christian denominations in the world. Only *some* of these are Lutheran. Do Lutherans think theirs is the only place God's people belong?

Not at all. Lutherans believe that they are part of the larger people of God. They *may* say that this or that reading of the Bible by another group may be incorrect. Lutherans are interested in being true; they are interested in truth and faithfulness. But they are not interested in being alone, in being the only true and faithful people. Wherever the love of God in Christ is taught and believed, there are the people of God, there is the church.

Lutherans know that some things they do result from who they are, from where and when they are. The Christians in South India or South Africa or South America—which include many Lutherans have different accents. As we shall learn, Lutherans believe people can be God's people without ever having heard the name of Luther or Lutherans.

What they do believe is that whoever they are, wherever and whenever they are, they are to be faithful. They are to grow in hearing and responding to the message of God. They believe that very rich treasures of grace have been given them. They want to be good stewards. They also want to spend those treasures on others. Since these are treasures of love and grace, they will never run out, but will only grow as they are put to use.

Lutherans cannot be the whole church, but they can be an inviting church. They speak not for themselves but for their God when they say, "You're invited. You belong here." They seek to be patient and understanding if you feel the call to go elsewhere. They only hope that you will not move yourself beyond the circle where the message of God reaches out, or beyond the people who respond in trust and faithfulness. They want you to use your mind to study this, in the name of the God who offers freedom along with love.

1. What does it mean to you that God is an inviting God?

2. What does it mean to you that this church is an inviting church?

3. Think of yourself as an inviting Christian. What are you like? How could you become more like this?

4. What is the main question or idea that remains with you at the end of this first session?

2
The Lutheran Heritage

THE CRITICAL QUESTION

Why bother with a heritage?

That's an important question to ask when you inquire about a Christian church body. Christianity was not invented today. It is a story covering two thousand years, but reaching far beyond that in years. Lutheranism was not invented today. It is a story about the Christian story, covering about five hundred years. Anyone who inquires about the Lutheran church today is necessarily exploring the Lutheran heritage.

Heritages come from the past. Most of the time historians keep the records straight. For this reason historians know many things you do not need to know to be a good Lutheran. They can tell you what kind of gowns preachers wore in Uppsala, Sweden, in 1638. They can tell you how people revised hymnbooks in Bremen, Germany, in 1755 or 1855. They keep the books on how Lutherans began work in today's Namibia a hundred years ago, or how they spread across North America during the past two hundred years. They have records on congregations, districts, denominations. Many of these records include inspiring stories of heroic and faithful people who lived the faith and died in faith; they also include many passages that even historians find boring.

To call a heritage a history lesson may turn off those who never did like history. After all, they are exploring a church, not a library. Other people use the word heritage in ways that prompt mixed responses. Heritages are antiques, and antiques fascinate some and repel others. Heritages may live in chests and chairs, but faith is more than furniture.

Why bother with a heritage? To begin to answer this question we can say: we *are* our heritages. We are the sum total of what our ancestors put into us. Some of it came through the genetic package that made us who and what we are. Some came through training. Grandparents taught us some of it. "That isn't done in our family," or "We Joneses have always been proud to do it this way," are typical ways of talking about heritages.

Some people want to join a church in order to forget heritages. They say you can have a direct and immediate experience of God and thus cut through all history. Yet the God we know comes to us in stories, and they are told by people. Some will say that the stories are about old traditions, and the traditions are dying. Forget them, some say. Yet even to forget a heritage means one has to know it first.

Yale historian Jaroslav Pelikan, who has taught many Lutherans how to think about heritages, tells the story of the choreographing of the play *Fiddler on the Roof,* which also became a movie. The play is about the heritage or tradition of Eastern European Judaism, which Hitler tried to destroy and which fades away as Jews build lives in Israel and America. The American choreographer Jerome Robbins was told that the play on which he would work was about the dissolving of a tradition. Robbins said, "Then the audience should be told what that tradition is."

While many details of the Lutheran heritage or tradition are forgotten, or being forgotten, or worth forgetting, it is not true that the Lutheran heritage is dissolving or disappearing as a whole. It is a growing reality among 80 million people today, and touches many who are not its members. Its story is worth learning in order to understand what it is that "isn't done in our church" and what "we Lutherans have always been proud to do this way."

Why bother with a heritage? Think of it not as a history but as a legacy, as a will. We bother with what comes from parents and grandparents because it enables us to live now and tomorrow; it enriches our ways; it gives us more possibilities. We open a vault to see what is there, and then we take what is there and reinvest it, spend it, draw security from it, serve as stewards of it. That's why we bother with a heritage. Moreover, in our case, we have to know not just that it is *there,* but, as Robbins said, we have to know what it *is.* Since the whole story takes libraries full, we can only draw a bold sketch.

THE PRESENTATION

The Lutheran heritage is a story. To study this story we can ask, first, What is the function of a story? One function is to inspire and entertain. Maybe some features of Lutheranism will do just that. There are examples of heroism, like the stories of Bishop Eivind Berggrav and Pastor Kaj Munk and Professor Dietrich Bonhoeffer, who resisted Hitler in Norway, Denmark, and Germany—or of many women, men, and children whose names we are just learning who have been tortured for their faith in South Africa. Such heroism inspires. There are probably plenty of funny moments in Lutheran heritages, too, as the monologues of Garrison Keillor of public radio's "A Prairie Home Companion" have taught millions in the 1980s. Yet one would not look to that heritage especially for laughs. We can make our inquiry class enjoyable, but it's too important to be dismissed as mere entertainment.

We present stories in order to learn who we are and what we stand for. Picture a young couple falling in love. They can talk for hours and hours, until their parents and friends think they are losing track of time and other realities. What are they doing? They are telling stories about heritages, in order to learn things about each other. Can you picture two lovers sitting down and asking each

other, "What are the fifteen principles by which you live?" or "Argue me into your philosophy!" Maybe we can picture a couple of philosophers doing so, and their eventual marriage just might be saved. More normally, we picture even the most philosophical lovers doing something else.

Lovers present themselves to each other as people with a story. "I was abused as a child; let me tell you about it." "I think you ought to know that I had a very unhappy love, and we broke an engagement." "My story? You may not enjoy it; you see I was married three times before, and. . . ." "I'd be glad to share with you my story; since my husband died, I've . . ." "I have to tell you all about my family. They don't want me hanging around with anyone who is not of our faith, or who makes less money than we do. We've always stuck together, and so I . . ." You can fill in the details.

Christian heritages have stories, and they are stories. The story of being a Baptist or Pentecostal in the Soviet Union is a story of dissent and suffering, perhaps of exile and persecution. The heritage of sixteenth-century Japanese Catholicism is one that includes tens of thousands being killed for their faith, tens of thousands being forced to turn against the faith and trample the images of Jesus and Mary. In African Lutheranism there is a heritage brought by missionaries but now transformed, as believers there shape the teachings in their own way for their own time and place. Some Lutherans have histories that stress doctrine, some stress piety, some stress works. They have certain things in common, and their stories need to be told for others to understand the question of identity—who Lutherans are, and the question of intention—what they hope to be and become.

For the moment, forget about the 2000-year Christian story. No, don't forget it; you can't forget it and be Christian, because God comes through story. Put it on the back burner for a moment while we tend to the Lutheran story bubbling up front. Then we will find that what the Lutherans are producing in five hundred years of their story is a way of serving up what has been produced for a longer period of time. It is also part of a menu to which others keep contributing. Let's examine the Lutheran part of this story.

One good place to begin with the Lutheran heritage is by talking about the person behind the name, Martin Luther. Perhaps we should say, "Ssshh! We have a scandal we have to talk about." Not that Luther lived a scandalous life. There are not many big offenses in his personal life, though some of his opinions will and should offend. No, by referring to a scandal we talk about the burden of being a body of Christians, and a movement, named after a person.

Everything has to be named something. United Methodists could have been Wesleyan, after John Wesley; their historians don't know quite what *Methodist* originally meant. Presbyterians are much more than people who are ruled by presbyters, or elders. It is very important to Episcopalians to be Episcopal, to be guided by bishops, but we need to know much more about them than that.

Luther said that he did not want a church named after him. Luther's enemies are the ones who named his fellow believers "Lutheran." So the "Lutherans" turned it around and made it a badge of pride. There was a time when "black" was a spiteful, taunting name, but people could not shake it. So Afro-Americans turned things around and said, "well, then, we'll be blacks. Black is beautiful." It went something like this with the beginning of the Lutheran heritage that we are now studying. Our Lutheran ancestors said, "Well, then, we'll be Lutherans. Luther stood for something beautiful."

Study Lutherans and Lutheran churches and you will find that most of them do not know much about Luther. This seems strange because he led a colorful life, and his 500th birthday party in 1983 was a time for film, television, book, magazine, and pageant treatment. Knowing his biography is not a ticket for membership or advanced standing. Lutherans are respectful of his achievement and admire it overall; but they respect and admire Saint Francis of Assisi as well. It is what Luther's life points to that mattered in the eyes of his enemies and eventually on the lips of his friends who accepted his name as part of their Christian identity.

If there were a *Who's Who in Germany* four or five centuries ago it might tell us that Martin Luther was born in 1483 and died in 1546. It would say that he was a monk, scholar, a professor of Old Testament most of his life, a preacher, a reformer, a husband and father. That he translated the Bible and wrote too much and made a lot of mistakes. That he centered his message in the grace of God, in faith, and in the use of the Bible. That a reform movement bearing his name spread around the world.

Luther was a religious genius, as even his enemies agreed when they called him "demonically" religious. He can be to religious experience and thought what Wolfgang Amadeus Mozart is to music, or Rembrandt to art, or John Milton to poetry, or Jane Austen to prose. He was by no means the only such genius. Nor was he in a class by himself. Nor was he best at all kinds of piety. But Luther was good at what we remember him for: encountering God, his own soul, and Scripture, and then, out of the torture of what he found in himself and out of the delight in what he found in God, experiencing grace and preaching it.

Luther felt—and Roman Catholic historians today would agree—that if God transacts with us freely and graciously, the church in Luther's day often obscured the transaction. There was plenty of truth available in the writings of the Roman church from that time. Yet this truth often became obscured. At Wittenberg, for instance, where Luther lived and taught, the civil officials were expert at collecting and parading relics of saints. People could buy rightness with God by patronizing the relics displays. Or there were peddlers of documents that people could purchase. These documents made for less punishment for themselves and others in the life to come.

Luther himself tried the way of pleasing God by punishing himself in the monastery. He remembered images in the Erfurt Cathedral—his home church—not only of a loving Jesus and Mary but also of Jesus the judge, sternly holding the sword in his mouth. Luther's God was not far away, silent, or absent, the way many people today—maybe you—have sensed God to be. Luther's God was too near, threatening, ready to send him to hell. He had to find and experience the loving and friendly face of God. As a teacher of the Bible—especially of Psalms, the book of Romans, and other books—he began to find that God never tired of searching for the human inquirer. And God's means were a tireless and spontaneous love, a never-ending grace, an eagerness to give a gift.

The central insight of Lutheranism is that our transacting with God centers not in our achievement but in divine grace.

God is not forced to give and we are not forced to receive. We are free to walk away from inquiry class and faith and church. If God were forced, or if we were, something would be lost. In fact everything would be. Neither does God sell grace. The Bible now and then uses the language of Jesus redeeming or buying back lost sinners, or it says that God bought us with the gift of Christ, though it leaves no room for us to buy God's favor. Yet to reduce the transaction to buying and selling would distort and cheapen—no, destroy—the nature of the way God acts toward us. So it is as a gift that God gives. Gift-giving is the way that shows and effects what God would do.

Luther insisted that God could be God only by acting freely and spontaneously, as one who shares love with people who cannot buy it or be forced to receive it or who do not deserve it. In turn, we could not respond to this God if we had to buy favors. The price would be too high, and our funds would be too tainted. The only response had to be like God's: free, spontaneous, and loving.

To further the Luther story, then, we turn to the heart of human response. If Luther used grace for God, he used faith for humans. Faith, he thought, was obscured by the church of his day because people were so busy working, earning, and thinking their way into God's favor. They could never satisfy their quest this way. There was another way, the way of faith. For Luther and Lutherans this means chiefly a trust or confidence in the God who makes promises. God is a faithful God. The Bible is a story whose plot tells of this faithful God dealing with people. And people need to respond with trust, or confidence.

Luther's struggle for faith continued throughout his life. When tempted to doubt or despair he could scribble, "I am baptized!" and thus remind himself that God had accepted him into the sphere of grace. Luther in his doubts and despairs might suffer, but his faith would then overcome his oppressive fears. Indeed, faith feeds on doubt the way fire feeds on fuel. For that reason, Lutheran Christians are taught not to be ashamed of their doubts, not to be overwhelmed. Even when they are not feeling faithful and forgiven of their sins, God is acting on their behalf.

To grace and faith we add a third key aspect of the Lutheran heritage. That word is *Scripture*, or *Bible*. It is impossible to make too much of Luther's and of Lutherans' devotion to the Bible, the ancient texts which they insist has to be the only source or norm for all Christian teaching. Luther made much of Scripture because, first of all, reading and experiencing it was the means by which he came to a new understanding of grace; it would work thus for others. Second, like all religious people he needed to address the issue of authority. On what grounds does someone teach something as true? On what basis does one risk life and eternity? On human wisdom? That was too shaky. On churchly authority like the Pope's

in his day? That, he thought, was corrupting and corrupt and, in any case, not fully biblical. On human reason? While Luther spoke out strongly against reason when it was used to gain God's favor, he cherished reason. But reason alone was weak; it could delude.

That left for him, and for Lutherans, the Bible, the Scriptures, where he was convinced that people hear the very word of God. He translated the Bible, knew huge chunks of it from memory, commented on it, preached it, taught it, helped the users of the new invention called the printing press disseminate it. In the next session we will go into detail about how Lutherans regard God's word, including the Bible. For now it is important to say only that it was the source and authority, vital because through it the Christian heritage or story comes to people in a new way. As Luther proclaimed his teachings, his part of the Reformation was underway, and he was making his contribution to Protestantism. The local church where inquirers now meet takes much of its tone and character from his experience four and a half centuries ago.

Someone has wisely said that the thoughts of a great Christian thinker or movement are not like pearls on a string. Snip the string, take a pearl off, tie the string, and you have almost the same thing you had before. No, instead, Christian thoughts are like rays that come out from the sun. The glowing core is the source of it all. For Luther and for Lutherans that is the story of a God who holds fallen humanity responsible, and then through the message of grace and the gift of faith, forgives sins and gives a new life. All Lutheran teaching eventually makes sense only as a corollary, as a ray of that glowing core.

THE STUDY

How do we get from there to here? A heritage is passed on from place to place, from generation to generation. Lutherans in Namibia, Argentina, Tokyo, and Atlanta do not have to learn the map of Europe to be Lutheran. But the map makes some contribution. By the middle of the sixteenth century the Lutheran reform was spreading through much of Scandinavia and Germany, moving into

Central and Eastern Europe, and elsewhere. By that time, however, Scotland, England, the Netherlands, France, other parts of Germany, and Switzerland were changing under the influence of other reformers; Luther's influence was more indirect, and sometimes other reformers disagreed with parts of it. Hence, the varieties of Protestantism we have today. But that is another story.

Most inquirers who use this manual are North Americans. While there was a stray Lutheran in Canada before the Mayflower, Lutherans know that America was settled more, and earlier, by other Protestants and Roman Catholics than by Lutherans. Scandinavians and Germans were fewer and later, and not until the nineteenth century did Lutheranism become America's third largest Protestant group. These latecomers, often rural and lower-middle-class city folk, did not, by and large, run things, though where they congregated very tightly, as in the Upper Midwest, there are exceptions. Some, like the Salzburgers driven to Georgia, had suffered for their faith in Europe. Others disagreed with trends in the state churches of Germany and Scandinavia and came for more religious freedom. Most came for economic reasons, to get a new start in the city and on the frontier.

They liked America, prospered, and grew in numbers. They started tens of thousands of congregations and numberless colleges, orphanages, hospitals, and agencies. They remain more northern than southern. There's a Lutheran belt running from New York, Pennsylvania, and New Jersey through Virginia west through Ohio to Missouri and, above it, the upper Midwest. However, modern mobility and efforts to spread the faith have led to the presence of some Lutherans almost everywhere. The vast majority are white, but Lutherans would like to see the body of nonwhite inquirers and members grow. Lutherans were divided into synodical bodies, thanks to the various ethnic groups and movements, divided leaders, geographical isolation, and other aspects of their heritage. These days they are working to reduce to two or three the major Lutheran bodies in the U.S. by the late 1980s. Differences among these bodies remain important to some leaders and members, but all the Lutherans agree to take their signals from some *confessions* or *creeds* written between the 1520s and 1580s, including the Augsburg Confession and Luther's Catechisms, among others. So they have basic agreement on matters of faith. Most are not disturbed by internal variety or pluralism. They think that Lutheranism should have different flavors in South Carolina and South Dakota, where it is a minority and where it is a majority, where it is "old-time" and where it is a new presence, where it is Hispanic and where it is Anglo.

There are some characteristic marks of Lutheranism. While many Europeans of Lutheran stock never became active in churches here, for the most part there are impressive stories of their fidelity to congregational life. They and their converts found that they truly belonged here, in America, in Lutheranism, in the congregations which they had helped form and where, they said, the Holy Spirit called them together.

They were adaptive to America. They are not sectarian. Some are not very ecumenical and have built barriers against joint activity with other Christians. But Lutherans have not built walls around church life as such. They think that Lutherans should talk and be involved with other church bodies and with the world.

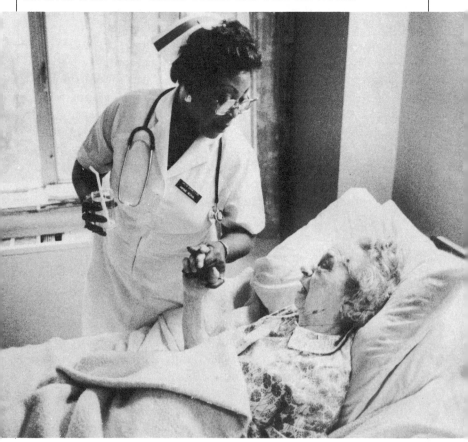

Overall, they have been better at activities of mercy than of justice. Other Protestants, Roman Catholics, and Jews, have more successfully taken risks in the public realm to try to bring about social and racial justice. Many Lutherans take part in movements of this sort, but others hold back. Yet these Lutherans often have good records for helping take care of the victims of injustice. They sponsor relief activities during and after wars, agencies for care of children and broken families, and institutions of healing. They expect such involvements to be signs that they are catching on to the good news of a God who acts and impels them to act.

Some Lutherans have had rather cramped and crabby views of life in God's universe. They will remember (and some still experience) strictness for strictness' sake. They were not supposed to engage in some worldly activities. For a variety of reasons, many chose to oppose social dancing, for instance. But today you will hear instead the language of moderation, restraint, balance, and personal discipline. Lutherans say we are to enjoy God's world and yet live in it with a moral seriousness that listens to the divine law. We are to relate our way of life to the human need around us.

Some of the "cramped and crabby" aspect was always countered by the fact that most Lutherans have enjoyed music, and many have supported other aspects of culture. Their colleges demonstrate the fact that, unlike some other Protestants, they have not been suspicious of artistic expression. They can use images in church, and let their music soar with their mentor Johann Sebastian Bach. They can have banners and murals, tapestries and posters, and see in them a delight in God's creation and human response.

SUMMARY AND REFLECTION

Lutherans do not have America or the world to themselves. They are not imperialists who think they have to conquer everyone in the name of Christ. They coexist and unite with nonbelieving citizens on civil and community causes. They are not as aggressive as some buttonholers and tract passers in evangelizing. Indeed, most of them could take lessons from Christians around them who understand better than they that faith no longer "comes with the territory." No longer—as it did in the Europe they left behind—can they count on being established by law and supported by the state. They have to help win loyalties of new people and are learning to do so. They want to welcome more inquirers.

They are not going to go into the business of Pope-baiting or Roman Catholic-hating. Nor are they going to put their first energies into knocking the literalists and fundamentalists on their right who, they think, often confuse the law of God with the gospel of grace. They will point out disagreements where these matter, and find fellowship where that is possible.

Lutherans are not to flaunt their banners as if they earned the love of God. Instead they are to enjoy their identity as Lutherans but walk humbly among other Christians. It would be a contradiction in terms to claim grace as an achievement, faith as a work, truth as something they discovered, instead of something that the Scriptures keep pointing to. When Lutherans are true to themselves, they remain inquirers, all their lives.

1. Why do you think a heritage is important?

2. Of the Lutheran teachings presented in this session, which means the most to you? Why?

3. When you consider the characteristics of the Lutheran church, as presented in this session, which attract you? Why? Which do you wonder about?

4. What does it mean to you that God is a gift-giver?

5. What is the main question or idea that remains with you at the end of this session?

3
God's Holy Word

THE CRITICAL QUESTION

How are we and God in contact?

That's an important question for anyone who wants to think about faith and about a church. The Lutheran version of the Christian faith wants to "let God be God." Those who speak in its name are not supposed to make things up. If you care about your destiny, you won't trust your future to fiction. You will not want people to preach to you that all will be well if they have no reason to say so except that they invented some.

Let God be God. It is possible to have something called a religion without God. Zen Buddhism and Taoism in Japan and China are examples, as are some forms of Unitarianism in America. Yet most of the time, when we talk about religion, we talk about people sensing some unseen power or force or person somehow acting upon them. They, in turn, must make some sort of response. The Christian faith is, in this sense, like many other religions. God is; God acts; God expects response.

This all sounds rather vague. More has been said about religion than about Christian faith. The opening paragraphs talk about "some" power "somehow acting" and wanting "some sort of response." They talk about "sensing." Made-up things do not help when one is deciding about destiny. Vagueness does not help either. A warm tingle in the toes or a breeze at one's neck is not a sufficiently clear signal that we and God are in contact. We need something more definite.

We need to have reasons to know that God is in contact with us. We can know something of this, perhaps, by thinking about our own heartbeats and other bodily processes. Somehow we are kept alive. Still, that is a too-vague basis for our relationship with God. After all, it could be that chemical interactions and physical mechanisms beyond our comprehension are simply doing their job. And in any case, the pump of a heart is not a very clear signaler of most things we want to know.

Are we alone in the universe? Is the universe nothing but a great silent accident? If so, there is no reason for God, faith, religion, the Christian church, or the Lutheran expression of the church. Our faith is based on the claim that we are not alone in the universe. We believe that God reaches across the silence and is in contact with us. We call that means of contact which Lutherans call "means of grace," the Holy Word of God.

THE PRESENTATION

Mention the word of God to Americans, particularly those of Protestant background, and they will immediately say "Bible." Most of them would use equal signs: word of God = Bible and Bible = word of God. Without doubt, the word of God and the Bible are completely and clearly entangled. But to use the equal sign is not wholly accurate, because more than the Bible is involved with the word of God. God uses a word to create the universe. Jesus Christ is the Word of God made flesh. The Bible itself makes these claims, so the equal signs will not work.

Having said this, however, let's proceed anyway to connect *Bible* with *word of God* long enough to get our thinking going. Lutherans do not believe that the story which saves them is available outside the Bible. There is no other plot out there that they are to learn about. They don't trust people who say, "I was talking to God the other day, and God told me . . ." If what they hear does not match what is in the Bible. They do not look for or reward private revelations. While people, including preachers, will and must apply the word to today's world, their basic story is the one recorded in the Bible.

How, then, should we think of the Bible? Lutheran Christians may not always use the comparison, but they think of it pretty much as a set of love letters from God. People who are apart and do not know of each other's existence cannot fall in love. Citizen

#43,5812,964 in the United States does not dream up citizen #19,262,894 in Argentina and fall in love with the idea of that number. There must be a someone; otherwise people only fall in love with love, or live with a dream. That's not enough to go on in matters of faith.

Now picture two people who come to know of each other's existence. This can happen sometimes only through letters. The newspapers now and then report on the marriage of two people who heard of each other across the miles and across the years. They began corresponding. They came to know each other. Perhaps they sent pictures to the one they came to love. Still, they had to get acquainted across distance. The page and the words on it expressed enough about each that they got a good idea of what the other was like. They came to trust each other. They were in contact.

What was said in those letters? It would not have been enough if each person had simply written "I love you" 50,000 times. A computer can do that in seconds or minutes. Long-distance lovers would tire quickly of such glib expressions. Mere sentimentality and the language of romance would not be the best way to build trust and love.

No, love letters include many other items. There are stories. We disclose ourselves to each other by telling what we have done, what people around us have done, and what we think about what they have done. Not all details are written to drive home the point "I love you." Most letters are more natural than that. The one who receives the letters wants to know everything possible about the other, but likes to pick it up through the casual clues that do not even have to be thought about. There is some waste space in most love letters. People repeat themselves. Perhaps they talk about business items. Yet one thing is clear. When the whole batch of letters is taken together, the one who receives them has been convinced: the sender loves me.

All comparisons have limits, but there are some good reasons to see the Bible as such a collection of love letters. Often enough it has God saying "I love you," for "God is love" is a frequent biblical assertion. But most of the time the Bible tells the story of God in the lives of people. On the hundreds of pages of Scripture we come to know a large cast of characters, not all of whom seem to have a lot to do with us or each other. Within those pages some business is transacted. And frankly—though it sounds irreverent to say—there is some waste space. Admit it: if you have ever tried to read the Bible in its entirety, you've encountered places that tell who begat whom, and they can be less than interesting. So you skip over them. That does not make the skipped passages something less than an aspect of the Word of God; we do not wish to reject a line of that batch of love letters. Yet some lines reach us more directly than others, in letters and in God's love letter, the Bible.

Love letters are words. They are not the person in a physical sense, up close. They reproduce the ideas of the beloved. Yet for people separated by distance, they are a great bridge. "Stay in touch," we say. Or, "You didn't write yesterday, and I felt out of touch, abandoned." Or, "It's as if you were right next to me; I can't wait until you will be." These are the kinds of things that come with the words on a page. The lover is disclosed and demands a response. We respond by reading the letters, replying, growing in love and changing our lives in light of what comes through the words. So it is with the way the Bible can work in us.

In our world, however, love letters are not only printed pages. We can speak them. While calling long-distance may cost more than postage, it is worthwhile to hear the voice of the other. If you have ever gotten or written love letters, or known someone who has, you will know that there are times when things get confused. "You sound so distant lately. How I'd love to hear your voice." And so one calls. Each can now get more clues: from the tone of voice, from the silences between sentences, from personal reassurances.

So it is with the word of God. In the Christian church—in the Lutheran church with special passion—people believe that the spoken word, often in the form of preaching, puts us in contact with God in a more vivid way. Martin Luther could be quite dramatic about this point. He made a German pun. Though he had great respect for the written word, he thought faith was built up more by speech. So he said the word should not be *geschrieben,* or written, but *geschrieen,* shouted. When the congregation gathers to learn of love and build up faith and hope, it comes to a church. Luther called the church "not a pen house but a mouth house." The pen is necessary to keep the story clear and true, but the mouth of a believing person was the best way to convey the word and love of God.

THE STUDY

The Lutheran Church is a church of the word. When it helps initiate people into God's family it baptizes. Then it says that it is the word that comes with mere water which gives power to the act. When it invites people to the Lord's table, it says that the word that comes with the bread and the wine empowers these earthly elements to be the agents of Christ's presence. That it values the spoken word—in preaching, teaching, and conversation—will be clear to anyone who spends five minutes on Lutheran soil.

To say that this is a church of the word is not to say that it is nothing but words, words, words. We want the gestures of love: the warm handshake, the arm around the shoulder in times of grief, the outstretched hand when we are hungry. Words can wear thin if they are not accompanied by actions. Instead, the word explains such gestures. Without it gestures can be confusing.

And certainly gestures do not tell all. We depend upon words to make things more clear. However, there can still be misunderstandings. People can evade the word. The comic W. C. Fields tried that on the Bible. He did not like its moral claims. He used to say, "I have spent a lot of time searching through the Bible . . . for loopholes."

It is also true that the same message in print or spoken word can be open to many interpretations. If this were not the case, there would not be so many church bodies. In many senses, denominations result from different interpretations of the same Scripture by people of good will, scholarship, and a passion to get things right. Yet having a script is better than not having one. Having Scripture provides the love-letter plot for most Christians. Having the spoken word based on that scriptural plot is the way most Christians find their faith made alive.

When Christians talk about their churches as churches of the word, they get used to seeing it live through word. Thus when a person is ill, the minister or some other representative comes to visit. They do not ordinarily bring along oils for healing. (Though mention of this symbol in the New Testament Letter of James is inspiring some Lutherans to return to the practice, and you may experience it. There is no magic in the oil; there is power in the words that go with it.) No, the agents of the church bring the word. They tell the story of God's love. They speak the words in which God addresses humans in need. They join with the ill person in speaking, in turn, to God, and thus keep the conversation, keep the word going. Has nothing happened to help effect healing? Yes, much has happened. Yet it has all been in the form of the word.

Lutherans believe that when the word is spoken something really happens. Let's put the next sentence in a curious form that still makes sense. When the word is spoken, something really happens: it does not *not* happen. People come to church or to other gatherings because when the word is spoken and believed, God is there. In Matthew 18:20 Jesus said, "For where two or three are gathered in my name, there am I in the midst of them." Of course, three people can sense the presence of Christ. But normally they gather and invoke his presence through the Word. Christ is the

Word. He comes to people through the Word they have read and the Word they speak. This is a clear signal of God's presence and power.

Teachers of preaching in Lutheran seminaries make an important distinction as they prepare a generation of speakers of the word. They define lectures and sermons in different ways. They show that when there is the preached or spoken word, something really happens; it does not *not* happen. In a lecture, one talks about God, one *describes* God. In a sermon one *offers* God and realizes the divine presence.

When we speak of the word of God, we connect it with all the acts and agencies of God. The Bible does this. By the word of the Lord the heavens were made: page one of the Bible, the book of Genesis, has God speaking a word and the universe comes from chaos to order. By the word of the Lord the prophets speak, judging Israel and giving us hope. Jeremiah 23:28 is helpful here: "Let the prophet who has a dream tell the dream, but let him who has my word speak my word faithfully."

To talk in such terms is to approach the word of God. But such talk does not say why there is a *Christian* church, a church devoted to Jesus Christ. In response to this question, we can use the same term: Jesus is the Word, the decisive and final word of God. This is the connection between the word of God and the Christian church. God is not saying something that is not revealed in Jesus Christ. When you read the New Testament you will not be able to find real differences between the terms *the word* and *the word of God* and, in Jesus' context, the *word of the Lord*. Jesus wanted it that way, according to the stories of him in the gospel.

Listen, in Luke 10:16: "He who hears you hears me, and he who rejects you rejects me, and he who rejects me rejects him who sent me." Jesus was not sending out the disciples to read Isaiah. He expected them to know Isaiah, as well as Jesus; and then the disciples were to evoke faith and the divine presence by telling of them, by bringing them to new gatherings of people. It all comes together in the first lines of John's gospel (1:1, 14): "In the beginning was the Word, and the Word was with God, and the Word was God. . . . And the Word became flesh and dwelt among us. . . we have beheld his glory, glory as of the only Son from the Father."

No wonder that a church that wants to be the church of the word must make so much of Jesus Christ as Word. This is especially important when we come to connecting the word with the book called the Bible.

Here, in our study, we should pause and point to a spectrum of ways Christians talk about the Bible and then point to characteristic Lutheran ways. There are extremes. There is an extreme liberalism that sees the Bible only as a great classic of literature. Among the great books, it might even be called *sacred* because so many people have given it so much respect. It can inspire nobler living.

At the opposite extreme are the literalists who treat the Bible the way Muslims treat the Qur'an, their sacred book. Muhammad claimed that this book was an utterance that simply came to him directly. It could not even be translated, since Allah spoke in Arabic. There could not be more than one interpretation (though, of course, there turned out to be; no two people even interpret a love letter quite the same way!). More moderate fundamentalism considers that God made use of human agency in giving the Bible. They would admit that the Bible's various books have differing literary styles, and even permissible errors in grammar. But they admit no errors in the original manuscripts, even when the Bible talks about such merely earthly affairs as science, geography, and history.

Since many Lutherans believe something like this about the Bible—and since many fundamentalists, evangelicals, and pentecostals of the sort one often sees on television propound this view, it is important to hear the case for it. The Bible only comes close, once or twice, to claiming that it is without error, and never exactly says that it is. But such interpreters use logic of this sort: the Bible is the Word of God; God, being perfect, cannot err, therefore the Bible is without error.

This concept of inerrancy is really a modern emphasis. It is a kind of Protestant counterpart to the Roman Catholic doctrine of papal infallibility. It is needed when the truth of Scripture is challenged. People want strong authority in their lives, and believe that the logic of inerrancy and infallibility will give it to them. They think that if they let go of inerrancy where the Bible and science seem to contradict each other, they will weaken in faith. How will one know that the disclosure of God can be relied upon? How can one have faith in the story if one can argue about its details?

In the history of the church, inerrancy has not been a very big point. For centuries, Roman Catholics did not make all that much of the Bible itself. When Protestants had a geographical territory to themselves—Lutherans in Germany or Scandinavia, Anglicans in England, Presbyterians in Scotland, Reformed in Switzerland—and never met other churches, they did not have to argue the authority of the Bible very much. Instead, they argued how to interpret it within, say, Lutheranism or Presbyterianism. It is only when Christians of one sort lived next to Christians of other sorts that they had to claim the Bible for themselves. There seemed no point in arguing about the Bible if it could have errors in it. So the logic of inerrancy developed further in the nineteenth century.

That those who believe in inerrancy get power from the belief is obvious: it is hard to criticize those who are so attentive to the biblical form of the word of God. Some Lutherans who have elevated this teaching may use it to decide who is a good Lutheran or a bad one. So it is useful to know about this teaching. Yet it is also important to see that this is not the decisively Lutheran way to talk about the word of God in connection with the Bible.

Most Lutherans like to remind people of what fundamentalists often overlook or cover up: that is, inerrancy solves little in respect to truth. Fundamentalists do not agree among themselves any more than do other Christians with differing views of Scripture. Some fundamentalists baptize infants and some only adults; some baptize by sprinkling, some by immersion under water. Some believe that Christ is really present in the bread and wine of the Lord's Supper and others consider bread and wine to be mere symbols. Some believe that Jesus will come to rule on earth for a thousand years and others do not. One could list hundreds of such points of disagreement among fundamentalists. Yet they all claim that they have an unerring hold on an inerrant Bible.

For these reasons we look elsewhere to find the decisively Lutheran understanding of the authority of the Bible. It should come as no surprise by now that such an understanding has to begin and end, not with logic or with one or two passages from the Bible, but with Jesus Christ, the Word of God. If the universe is not silent but God speaks, and if God climaxes this speaking in Christ the Word, then the book of God, the Word in the form of the book, must be seen in the light of the way it relates to Christ.

For a brief moment let's turn our attention to a textbook, one that came from a conservative professor at a conservative seminary of a conservative Lutheran body. Frederick E. Mayer was comparing teachings of all the major religious groups in a book called *The Religious Bodies of America* (Concordia, 1954). When he came to Lutheranism he stressed the Lutheran principle of *sola Scriptura,* that is, "Scripture alone." The Lutheran statements of faith have "no interest in an atomistic, proof-text, concordance approach to the Scriptures," which means an approach that cuts them up into small parts and puts them back together in a way that pleases people with scissors, microscopes, and pastepots. Here is Mayer saying what Luther and formal Lutheran teaching through the centuries have said so clearly:

"The Lutheran Confessions [creed statements] take for granted that a Christian accepts the Scriptures as God's Word, both as God speaking in this Word here and now and as God's Word spoken in times through the holy writers. In Lutheran theology [religious thought] *the believer does not accept the absolute authority of the Scriptures as an* a priori *truth* [based on a theory], *but because he [or she] has learned to know Christ as his [or her] divine Savior; has experienced the power of His Word in the Scriptures upon his [or her] heart; and relies implicitly on Christ's own statements concerning the divine character of the Scriptures.*" [Italics added].

That paragraph is more condensed and more formal than most of those in this manual, but its lines are worth going over a few times. Luther was an extremist in expressing this same view. "Whatever does not teach Christ is certainly not apostolic even though St. Peter or St. Paul teach it. Again, whatever preaches Christ is apostolic even though Judas, Annas, Pilate, or Herod [the New Testament villains] might say it." Again: "Whatever communicates Christ is true and acceptable." Luther liked to say that the Bible "presses" or "pushes" Christ, that it is the manger in which Christ lies. He even pressed or pushed the plot of Jesus back into the Hebrew Scriptures which we call the Old Testament. So did the New Testament. Jesus was foreseen in Isaiah's figure of the suffering servant, or the Exodus' image of a serpent on a pole in the wilderness. That is why Christians read the Hebrew Scriptures differently than do Jews. And Luther sometimes was more reckless than most modern Lutherans about some stories, and even some whole books, of the Bible. He did not think the Letter of James, though it was written by Jesus' own brother, to be on a par with others because it did not "communicate Christ."

ϨΟΤΟΥϢϤΕΠΕϤΕΝΕΛΛΛΤΕ
ϨΜΠΕΣΪΚΪΟΣΕΝ Ϯ̄ΛΥΝ̄Σ· Ν̄
ϤΡΟΥΧΕΝΛΪΕΠΥ̣Λ̄Λ̄Λ̄Ϥ
ΛΣΠΛΖΕΝ̄ΝΕΤΣΡΗΟΠ· ΛΤΩ
ΛΜϨΩΚΕΠΛΛΟΠΠῩΝͲϨ̄Ρ
ΠΡΟΦΗΣΟΠ̣ΛΛ̣Ε̣Λ̄ΝΣ̄ΝΟΥ̣
Ν̄ΖΗͲϤ̣ : ···   ····· ···· ····

ΠΟ Ͳ̄ΛϨΕΝΛΟΓΟΣΕΝ̄ΤΑ̣ΡΙΕΛΥΝ̄ΤΟΥ
ΛϪΙΑΡΤΟΝΩΝ̄ ΤΟ̄ΤΕΤΟΟ̄ΤΠΛΤΕ
ΣΛΖΟͲΕΙΜΕΣΤΕΧΕΛΥϤΕΠΗ̄ΤΝ̄
ΚΝΓΑΡ̄ϮΛΙΕΤΛΧΕΕΙΣΤΛΙΝ ΝΛΪΝΗ
ͲΝ̄ΧΕΜΕΥϪΛ̄Γ̄Ϥ ΕΤ̄Ν̄Τ̄ΝΕϤ̄ΤΕ
Π̄ΙͲΖ̄ΟϢ̄ΡΖΙΣΕΝΗΤΝ̄ ΕΠ̄ΠΝΛῩΜΩϤ
ͲῩΓ̄ΝΟΪΝΛΟΓΟΣ ΕΤΑͲΙΣ̄ΤΕΤΟΟͲΤ̄Ν̄ΤΕΤ̄Ϋ

ΕΥϢΕΚΟϢϢϢϤΛΣΕΝΛͲΕΦΩΚΗ̄
ΠΕΪΜΛΣͲΗΡΙΟΝ· ΛΠΩΘΙΚΩΝ
Ν̄ϢϢΠΗΡ ΕΝ̄Π̄ΝΛῩΤΕΡΟΣΕΝ̄ΤΕΤΟΠ
ΟͲΣΙΛΕῩΛΣ̄ϢϢΠΕ̄ΣϨΟΛͲ̄Ν̄
Φ̄ΟΟΡͲΠ̄Π̄ ͲΕΤͲΜΕ· ΖΟͲΛΝΣΕ
ΕῩϢϢΛΝ̄ΕΙΕͲΛΚΜΗϢΛΥϢϢΣΕΕΚΟΡ
Ν̄ΘΙΠΕΣΠΕΡΜΛ· Ν̄ΤΕ̄Π̄ΝΟΣΕΠΙ
ΜΛͲ ϢϢΛΡΕͲΟϢΝΕΛΙΝͲΘΟΜ̄
Μ̄Φ̄ΟΟΡͲ· Φ̄ΟΟΡ̄Ͳ̄Γ̄ΩΩϢϢΛΥ
ΧΙΝͲΟΟΜ̄Ν̄ͲΟϢΜΕΕΡΟΥ· ΖΩΣ·
ΕϤ̄ΕΠΣΠΕΡΜΛ̄Ρ̄ΕΝΕΡͲΕΪΠ̄ΤΛΪ·
ΕͲͲΕΠ̄Λ̄ΠΜ̄Σ̄ͲΗΡΙΟΝΝ̄ΤΟΥ
ΝΟͲΛΛΕ̄ΤΕΪΡ̄ΕΝΛΛΟΥΪΝΟͲΩͲ·
ΧΕΚΛΛΣΕΝ̄ΕͲΟ̄ΕΙϢ̄Μ̄Φ̄ΝΣΕ·
Ρ̄ΛΣ̄ΧΗΜ̄ΟΝῙΝ̄ΝΛϢϢΝ̄ΛΛ̄Ε̄Ρ̄ΧΟ
Ν̄ΤΛΝϢϢΦΩΚΣΕͲ̄Ν̄ΝΛΪ· ΠΩͲΛ
ΡΛῙΠΟͲΛΙΜΟΟͲΥϮ̄ Ν̄ΠΕϤ̄ΧΠΟ·
ΗΣΤΕΤ̄Ρ̄Ν̄ΝΛͲΣΟΟͲΝΗ̄Π̄ϮΖΩϤ
ΕῩΧΕϢϢΟΟͲΠ̄Ν̄ΛΛϢϢΛΝ̄Σ̄ΩΚͳ
ΛͲϢϢΝ̄Ν̄ΛͲΝΛϢͳΕ· Ν̄ΖΟͲΟ ΔΕ
ΖΛΜΠΣͲΗΡΙΟΝΕͲΟΥΛΛΝΕ
Ν̄ΤΕΠ̄ΝΛΛΟΓΟΣΕΝ̄Ν̄ῙΖ̄ΚΗͲΕ·
ΟΠϢ̄ΟΝΟΝΧΕΕͳΠΙΣΩ̄ Τ̄Ν̄
ΛΛ̄ΛΛ̄Ν̄ΣΕΝΛͲ· ΕͳΚΕΠΛΪ·

There is one other distinctive Lutheran view about God's Holy Word. Other Christians also teach this view, just as they teach that the Bible gets its authority from Christ and not vice versa. Yet Lutherans like to claim a kind of patent on this understanding from the time of the Reformation. You will often hear them speaking about how to distinguish *law* from *gospel* as word of God. Everyone recognizes that the Bible is full of laws and full of the law of God. Everyone recognizes that it is full of gospel, the good news of what God does in Christ. How do these relate?

The law in the Bible is the set of words that does two things. It is first of all the way God orders the world, keeps the creation from being destroyed, and keeps chaos from overwhelming us. From its model we get human government and law. Second, in the believer's life, the law of God in the Bible drives home the point that the God of the Holy Word is holy and humans are not. It convinces sinners that they are sinners. It devastates any who thought they could be right with God on the basis of keeping the law, because it shows how impossible such an effort would be. It drives a person to depend upon God who has another word, a word of grace, of good news, of forgiveness, of gospel. "Law came in, to increase the trespass" (Romans 5:20) is a favorite way to say and see this aspect of the law.

Paul goes on, "But where sin increased, grace abounded all the more, so that, as sin reigned in death, grace also might reign through righteousness to eternal life through Jesus Christ our Lord" (Romans 5:20-21). All Christians believe this, but no one wants to be clearer about this distinction or shout it louder than Lutherans. The gospel shows us the distinction between sin and grace and tells how God is a God of grace, writing love letters to us about a love that God shows in Jesus Christ. In the Hebrew Scriptures, before Jesus came into the world, this loving, gracious face of God was also shown; but now it is revealed decisively in the face and fact of Jesus Christ, the Word of God. The Bible, then, gets its authority from the gospel, the good news, which most emphatically gets called "the Holy Word of God."

So we have this library of 66 books now called the Old and the New Testaments. They are to be the only source and norm of Lutheran teaching. You cannot get away with something by saying "it's the tradition of the church" or "it's doctrine" unless you can show how it issues from the Word of God in Christ, witnessed to in the Bible. You will not settle all arguments because you claim the Bible; even members of a church body have arguments while they claim to be in agreement. But you will know that you have to make an appeal to the Bible or have your teaching issue from it to get the argument started, or, possibly, ended. You will not hear a Lutheran sermon based on a text from anything but the Bible. You will not hear Lutherans simply placing the Bible on a shelf of sacred books, though it also belongs there. You will hear them urging you to "search the scriptures, because you think that in them you have eternal life; and it is they that bear witness to me" (John 5:39). You will also be urged a verse further, to hear the chiding and the call to decision for those who have searched the Scriptures, "Yet you refuse to come to me that you may have life" (John 5:40).

We go to Christ the Word of God to receive God, truth, and life.

SUMMARY AND REFLECTION

"The Bible is an unfinished plot, and you are in it." Someone has said this about the Scriptures, and voiced a point that squares with the Lutheran teaching. The Bible in the Lutheran church is not an old sacred classic, a basis for argument, a way to start or settle church fights, or a library for scholars only. The Bible is a set of love letters that express the character of God who acts and speaks. It calls forth response.

To say that the Bible is an "unfinished plot" is not to say that believers expect new books to be added to it. Theoretically it would be possible to add books. The early church set the *canon*, the rule by which the books were chosen (the word is also used to refer to the chosen books themselves). It was a bit nervous about including some of the books, and for a few hundred years some believers thought that some rejected writings belonged in the Bible. Yet the canon, while being open, as Lutherans teach, it not likely to be added to. And what we have is so long and rich and complex that no scholar exhausts even a few pages of it. The Bible and the preaching, teaching, praying, and conversing based on it speak to the heart.

By the power of the Holy Spirit we come to believe in the word of God.

To speak of the unfinished plot, then, is to see that the gospel is for you. It addresses you. You could write your name in a wide-margined Bible wherever it uses the word *you* and you would be in the plot, and accurate about its purpose. When you pass it on by communicating Christ, you are responding. You are being faithful to the story and the spirit of the gospel. You may have an impediment in your speech, or use sign language or braille, or your grammar may not be perfect. But you will be uttering the word of God. To do so is a responsibility, a terror, a thrill, a promise. And the word of God is never vain or void. It achieves God's purposes. It awakens faithful response, it inspires hope, it empowers love.

1. What does it mean to you that God is a God who makes contact with you, sends a "love letter" to you?

2. How do you respond to the Lutheran view of the word presented in this session?

3. What does it mean to you that God's word is "for you" and for you to pass on?

4. What is the main question or idea that remains with you at the end of this session?

4
A Creed for Life

THE CRITICAL QUESTION

Do I have to believe *that*?

Inquirers sometimes ask this question about teachings of the Christian faith. They know that whole libraries about doctrine exist. They have perhaps glimpsed shelves of books about creeds in the studies of ministers or in church libraries. They have some sense that, lurking in the background, there is a long list of dogmas that they will have to agree to. It is true that doctrine often has a bad name: the Christian church has often misused creeds, enforcing consent with them rather than letting them give life and identity. So it is natural to be hesitant.

The question, Do I have to believe *that*? so often focuses on the *that*, on some strange teaching. Then it is easy to forget the verb. Try another focus: Do I *have* to believe that? Here we can make some distinctions. A creed is not just for making commands or providing heresy-hunters with weapons. The word *creed* comes from the Latin word *credo*, which means "I believe." Since the Christian creed is to grow like rays of the sun out of the gospel of Jesus Christ, belief in this creed is also a gift. We could better say, Do I *get* to believe this? In a way, creeds function less to say, "This we must believe in order to be considered Christian," and more to say, "This is what we believe because we are Christians; you will never understand us if you do not hear us saying this."

One could go even further and say that in the Christian church it is not *what* you know but *who* you know that matters. The quality of Christian life is not measured by seeing which people pass a final examination with the most knowledgeable answers to questions about the faith. God measures the quality of Christian life by our closeness to God's way, to the love of Christ, and by the power of the Holy Spirit in our lives. The creeds basically outline and reinforce our trust in the Who or the One we know and in whom we believe. With this approach to the creeds we present one creed, the Apostles' Creed, and one angle on it, from Luther's Small Catechism.

THE PRESENTATION

The Apostles' Creed is a brief document that most Christians know from memory. It is one of two creeds that most Lutherans recite to display, confirm, and strengthen their faith in main services of worship. (A third creed, the Athanasian Creed, is accepted by Lutherans but rarely used in Lutheran worship.) While it echoes the teaching of the early New Testament apostles, it took form gradually. No one called it the Apostles' Creed until almost A.D. 400. Yet it condenses well the main themes of biblical faith, and serves well our presentation of that faith in a Lutheran context.

Mention of the Lutheran context leads to another document, Luther's Small Catechism. This is a short tract, a pamphlet so small you could quite easily lose it between weeks if you consult it in inquiry classes. Luther knew enough about us to know that we weren't all going to huddle in libraries learning doctrine. He wanted a book profound enough that a professional theologian like himself could study it throughout life, but simple enough that individuals, families, and local churches could use it. It is probably the most widely used statement of Christian faith as Lutherans know it.

Now let's think about the function of a creed and a catechism. A story will help to show us how they fit into Christian faith and life.

A man was hit by a streetcar, back in the olden days of streetcars. A crowd gathered. It was clear he was desperately hurt, and someone summoned help. While it was coming, a young priest happened by, wearing a cassock. The doctor also arrived, and said, "It's too late for me to do anything, Father. You take over. You'd better administer the last rites" (the Roman Catholic ritual for those near death). The priest got out his black book and a kit of things he needed in such emergencies. He was going to go by the book. To the barely conscious man he whispered urgently, "My son, are you of the Catholic faith?" The man nodded. "Do you know you are a sinner?" Another nod, as energy ebbed. Then came the question that is central in the creed: "Do you believe in the Holy Trinity, the Father, the Son, and the Holy Spirit?"

With the strength of a last gasp the man breathed: "Say, what is this, Father? Here I am dying, and you want to run me all the way through the catechism?"

The dying man knew more than did the priest about the when and where of the creeds and catechisms. The point of the story: never think that what you know and how many things you know are tests of Christian faith and life.

The positive place of creeds becomes clear when we see how they work outside the circle of faith. Americans have a kind of informal creed in the second paragraph of the Declaration of Independence. "We hold these truths to be self-evident, that all men are created equal . . . ." Not all the world accepts this self-evidence. But Americans take it on faith and then try to put it to work in life. Or people may say of a coach that he or she lives by a certain credo. Winning is everything, or winning isn't everything, or the best offense is a good defense, or the best defense is a good offense, or sport builds character, or it is not building character that counts, but winning games. We learn to know people in light of their credos, and we learn to expect certain kinds of action because of what they say.

A creed also provides a certain structure for faith. Our minds are such that things stick there better if those things are ordered. A story has to have a plot if we are to grasp and keep it. The Apostles' Creed, with its three *articles* or clusters of themes, provides such an outline.

Similarly, a catechism like Luther's orders faith in a question-and-answer form. Luther divided faith into chief parts. This creed, with his explanations, is the second part (after the Ten Commandments, which we will study in the next session). He followed the Ten Commandments and the Apostles' Creed with explanations of the Lord's Prayer, Holy Baptism, and Holy Communion—an order we will follow in our own inquiry.

THE STUDY

"I believe in God, the Father . . .
"I believe in Jesus Christ . . .
"I believe in the Holy Spirit . . ."

Thus begin the three articles of the Apostles' Creed. These beginnings are clues to a three-fold division within Christian faith. They are also references to God called by the names Christians use: the *Trinity,* or the *triune*—the three-in-one—God. If you do not understand everything about the Trinity, do not feel bad. One of the greatest Christian thinkers, Saint Augustine, admitted that we use the word *Trinity* only because we have to say something, and this word is better than silence. We have to say something, and this word has grounds in New Testament ways of speaking. We have to say something, and this word adapts to the thought patterns of various ages. For instance, we are not likely to be able to think exactly the way the Greeks thought when most creeds were written.

Yet we have to say something to protect ourselves from saying other, and wrong, things. Since this is language about God who is boundless, and in many ways not knowable by our limited human minds, we reach for the best we can, and this word *Trinity* will do.

Not everyone likes the language of the Trinity. President Thomas Jefferson judged it to be mathematics, not religion. The story is told that a person in Japan, hearing about the Father, Son, and Holy Spirit, asked the missionary, "So, then, do you believe in three gods?" "No, in one," replied the missionary. "Ah, then," the Japanese person responded, "I see that you are ruled by a committee." This person's confusion is understandable. We can address it, and perhaps our own confusion, by asking why the creeds talk this way about God.

The God who addresses us through the Holy Word needs a name, and gets many. Ancient Hebrews felt God's name was too holy to be uttered, and found clever ways to avoid using the name of God that they knew. You have probably overheard worshipers or users of modern Bible translations talking about *Yahweh,* which is one way God was disclosed: "I AM WHO I AM" or "I WILL BE WHO I WILL BE," but it was never uttered by ancient Hebrews. We Christians inherited this and other names for God, but we had a special problem.

Here it is: Christians are *monotheists.* They do not believe in a universe of spirits, one of whom is higher than the others. Rather, Christians believe that God as Being or as Person is set apart in kind and quality from beings and persons, be they in the spirit or physical world. Moreover, all things come from and go to this God.

Next, Christians witness to the power of God in Jesus. They call him "the Son of God." For instance, in a very early writing, Paul's letter to the Colossians (1:15, 18-19) we hear typical words about Jesus: "He is the image of the invisible God, the first-born of all creation; . . . He is the head of the body, the church; . . . For in him all the fulness of God was pleased to dwell." The church has spent many centuries witnessing to this fulness of God in Jesus.

The church could not downgrade Jesus to merely human status; yet it could not worship two Gods. What is more, it witnessed that the word of God and the word in Christ were made present through a "person" that the Bible called the Spirit of God, the Holy Spirit, the Spirit of Christ. So Christians used the language of "the three-in-one and one-in-three," the Trinity. Such language holds together faith in one God alone and in three "persons"—Father, Son, and Holy Spirit. One way to begin to make sense of the Creed and the Trinity is to take the articles and persons in a sequence.

"I believe in God, the Father almighty, creator of heaven and earth."

To begin let's briefly discuss an issue that is an important one in our generation: the use of masculine language for God. There is no doubt that the Bible ordinarily refers to God with masculine images and names. Furthermore, some people have used such biblical references to keep women down. In response, others want to remind us that God is more than our pronouns, more than our genders. Indeed, the Bible often ascribes powers to God that women possess: the power to give birth to Israel, and to nurse Israel. Changing the language of liturgy and of Bible translation is one creative way people are addressing this issue. You will probably find a variety of opinions on the subject in any circle of inquirers.

For now it is important only to note that many Christians, and many Lutherans, are nervous about actually changing words of the Bible in translation to "make it come out right." Many feel it is better to keep the text as it has come to us. Then, in our preaching, teaching, and conversation, we can explain the limits of exclusive masculine language and images for God. Then we can be liberated both to hear the Scriptures and the creeds, and to share in reconceiving ways to talk of God, ways that help liberate both women and men.

Now for our study of the way the Catechism explains these words. It accents not the fatherhood of God, except to say that God does things for us "out of fatherly and divine goodness and mercy." More than this, the Catechism stresses that what matters about God is being the Maker or Creator of heaven and earth. But the words here do not dwell on the God who made the ever-expanding universe. This universe, about which scientists are learning and teaching us more and more, allows for an ever-greater concept of God and of the power of the divine Word that created. But even this is not the main point.

Instead, everything comes home at once to the person who utters the creed, to the person who is inquiring about faith. "I believe that God has created me and all that exists." The original languages say that God "created me *along with* all that exists." This version provides an important clue. Our destiny is tied up with that of nature and other beings. We are not alone. We are not proud egos, free to do what we want with earth, air, and water. We share their destiny. Blow them up, pollute them, or foul them, and we die. The Creator has something else in mind.

According to Lutheran understandings, creation can mean two things. First, God made things out of nothing. The Bible does not often talk about this theme, but it is an important one. It points to the spontaneity of God, the divine power, the love that looks for relation. God wanted something where there was nothing, and spoke, and it was. Second, creation means that God keeps on making things, God keeps on creating order where there was chaos. Genesis 1:2, not very far into the Bible, points to this. The whole of the Bible talks frequently about this way of creating, and so does Luther's explanation of the Creed. We are participants, under God and with God, in the continuing creation that we see in mothering and fathering, in inquiry groups, in the work of artists and politicians, whenever they preserve and extend creation.

God "has given me and still preserves my body and soul with all their powers." The words go on to say that God provides me with all that I need and that he protects and guards me. *Me. I.* Is the creed appealing to the ego, and is its explanation creating new narcissism for life in continuing "me decades"? Not at all. Here, as always, it is a God-centered faith. But now we see what kind of God we are praising. God is a God who, while busy creating a universe, creating order out of chaos, cares enough to focus on you.

This is the astonishing point: creation is all personalized; it is "for you." This point runs through Christian faith as Lutherans understand it. We know the world through our eyes, ears, senses, and mind. We live out our lives in the sight of the God who has given and preserves them. God places us as stewards of the earth. The earth comes to us as a set of almost limitless possibilities. If two players wanted to make all the possible moves on one chessboard, it would take them and some partners—all the people who

ever lived—trillions of years. Life has even more possibilities than those on one chessboard. God places us in the midst of life to deal with some of these possibilities. We do not become gods because God lets us create, but we do carry on godly activity when we produce a child, or a pot, or a poem, or a product.

It must be said, however, that Lutherans cannot help but sneak in their view of our human limits. "I do not deserve it," Luther writes. Rather than grovel, however, or go on about how sinful we are, the short text in the Catechism hurries to a climax: since I do not deserve it, "Therefore I surely ought to thank and praise, serve and obey" God. Everything that we say about creation and goodness appears against the backdrop of human limits. It is said knowing that God is eternal, but the world is not. We are aware that the good creation, for reasons we do not and cannot understand, also has cancer cells, fanatic militarists, exploiters of the poor, and earthquakes that destroy. The Bible does not allow that these come from some other God or near-God (for Satan, the Bible's personified force of evil and rebellion is by no means near-God). Nor does the Bible show a powerless God. Instead, it regularly depicts a God who suffers with the people, who is at their side, who weeps with them and comforts them as a participant in suffering, not as an aloof sovereign.

The Second Article of the Creed focuses on the second person of the Trinity, Jesus Christ. We will concentrate on Luther's explanation, a sort of Lutheran creed. Lutherans are so taken with this passage, and so focused on the work of Christ, that some critics have accused them of being unitarians of the second person of the Trinity. But Lutherans are not and do not want to be viewed as such. They want theirs to remain a God-centered faith. Yet they find good reason to grow poetic when it comes to the person and work of Christ.

This is a good place to make a point about a characteristically Lutheran way of thinking. When Martin Luther was in the monastery he thought much about *divine election*. This is the teaching that says that those who are saved are saved because God elects them. Many believers reverse this teaching and say, then, maybe God didn't elect them. How could they know if they were elect? Luther went to his confessor, his confidant, to whom he could tell his doubts and fears. The confessor saw that the young monk was troubled because he was dealing with mysteries and difficulties beyond human knowledge. He must ask a different question. He must change the plot.

The confessor said: start at another place. You cannot know what is going on in the mind of God. You are not God. You can only know and see what is going on in the story and in the wounds of Christ. You are told by the gospel that his death is for you. Reason back from that story. Reason back from the sight of Jesus

THE SECOND ARTICLE

I believe in Jesus Christ, his only Son, our Lord.
He was conceived by the power of the Holy Spirit
and born of the virgin Mary.
He suffered under Pontius Pilate, was crucified, died, and was buried.
He descended into hell.
(Or, He descended to the dead.)
On the third day he rose again.
He ascended into heaven, and is seated at the right hand of the Father.
He will come again to judge the living and the dead.

What does this mean?
I believe that Jesus Christ—
true God, Son of the Father from eternity,
and true man, born of the Virgin Mary—
is my Lord.

At great cost
he has saved and redeemed me,
a lost and condemned person.
He has freed me
from sin, death, and the power of the devil—
not with silver or gold,
but with his holy and precious blood
and his innocent suffering and death.

All this he has done that I may be his own,
live under him in his kingdom,
and serve him in everlasting righteousness, innocence, and blessedness,
just as he is risen from the dead and lives and rules eternally.
This is most certainly true.

on the cross to whatever you can learn about a loving God. Don't reason in the other direction. Ever after, Lutherans got into the habit of looking at Christ, at the wounds of Christ, to learn what they need to know about how God acts toward them.

Here's how God acts: "I believe that Jesus Christ—true God, Son of the Father from eternity. . . ." This statement maintains the Bible's witness to the way the fulness of God lives in Jesus Christ. He is also "true man, born of the Virgin Mary." Whenever we wish to think about what God does in Jesus we know that a key element in the transaction is that Jesus is our representative. A holy God could not tolerate the way we spoil the world and our lives and God's way. In the Christian story, Jesus stands in our place and suffers all that the world and our sins could heap on him, to the point of death.

Some early Christians, known as *Docetists,* did not like to think that Jesus was "true man," who cried and sweat and died. They invented the notion that he was a phantom or a fantasy that only seemed to be human, while Jesus who was the Christ stayed divine. Such an understanding ruins the whole transaction. One who represented humans had to be human. He was born of the Virgin Mary. Lutherans have had no argument with Roman Catholics over this role of Mary. They witness to the virgin theme as a way of saying that God draws a veil over the special way Jesus was and is among us.

He is "my Lord." This means that I surrender to him. It does not mean that he will be authoritarian or totalitarian. He tells us often enough that his lordship is liberating, that he would serve and have us serve.

The words go on to say that Jesus saved us at "great cost." He bought us back from the slavery we all feel—to the bottle, to our emotions, our temptations, our meanness, "the devil"—with "his holy and precious blood and his innocent suffering and death." This is the plot of Good Friday, about which Christians sing in sorrow.

The intimate note sounds again. Jesus Christ did all this suffering and he died "that I may be his own." Here's another love letter. To belong to him means a surrender of whatever it is that keeps me from the ways of God. It does not mean that I have no personality or freedom. Indeed, now, I get to "serve him in everlasting righteousness, innocence, and blessedness."

We pause a moment here. It may seem strange that the last three big words come up in Lutheranism, a form of Christian faith sometimes faulted for its low view of human nature. In a competition to see who can paint the lowest picture of human beings, Luther might win. For him, even the pious prayers of someone who wanted to earn God's favor were bad. Even the spiritual life was a problem. The language of original sin comes naturally to Lutherans. So how can Lutherans talk about "righteousness, innocence, and blessedness?"

Here we plant another flag with a Lutheran mark on it. As always, you don't *have* to be Lutheran to believe this, but you *get* to have this view nurtured if you are a Lutheran believer. Just as we cannot say enough about our limits apart from God, so we Lutherans cannot say enough about our limitlessness under God, in Christ. Luther's formula was that we are "at the same time righteous and sinners." This side of death, we never leave being a sinner behind. Yet we are also righteous. What Jesus did to represent us pleased God. Now God looks at us not always or only as our old selves. Indeed, so vivid is our identity with the act of Jesus that when God looks at the baptized, at people who live in faith, God sees them as faithful. Luther can be extreme on this point: we are not to be only "as Christ," but we are to be "a Christ" to the neighbor. We are thoroughly guilty on our own; we are thoroughly innocent as we are identified with Christ. We never stop being sinners, but that is seeing us only from one angle. We are also always able to be saints alive, when viewed from the other angle.

This witness allows us to look ahead. The New Testament faith is based on Jesus' rising from the dead. Without that faith, we would be of all people the most miserable. Christians believe that in the rising again of Jesus, in the event we call Easter or the Resurrection, something really happened. It did not *not* happen. This means, Jesus' rising was not just a change in the psychology of the forlorn disciples who gave up hope and then "experienced" him.

Instead, God worked something new in Jesus. He became present again, and remains so, Christians believe, when they are gathered in his name; when they celebrate his Supper; when his word is preached and believed. So they shall serve him forever, rising "just as he is risen from the dead and lives. . . ." Lutherans are not much interested in the Shroud of Turin or scientific evidence of Jesus' rising. They do not usually spend a lot of time arguing about evidence for an empty tomb, or speculating about Jesus' appearances after the Resurrection. They cherish the stories in the New Testament and are moved by faith.

What convinces them is that people live by this faith, their changed lives are witnesses to the risen Jesus. That's how it worked in the Acts of the Apostles, in which no one waved shrouds of Turin or talked about corpuscles and cells being revived. They talked about the new thing God was doing in the new age begun with Christ's rising.

The Book of Acts is an early history of the people who did this talking and living. They could say, as the Apostles' Creed does, "I believe in the Holy Spirit; the holy catholic Church. . . ."

Luther's explanation does not startle us at first. We read: "I believe that I cannot by my own understanding or effort believe in Jesus Christ my Lord, or come to him." Now take out some words, and it does shock: "I believe that I cannot . . . believe." I cannot believe, since I have nothing but my understanding and effort to help me, and I believe they do not count. Faith is a mystery, as every inquirer knows and learns. Two people can study the same doctrines, go to the same university and study the same philosophy, and face the same kind of threatening illness. One will believe and the other will not, despite equal application of "understanding and effort."

Are we sounding like "divine election" people who really believe in fate, that whatever will be, will be? No, but we are out to protect the claim that faith is a gift, that it is the gracious act of God through and as the Holy Spirit. We do not get to claim faith as our achievement. Bumper stickers and tracts today often claim or imply that it *was* "through my own understanding and effort" that I came to believe. In truth, I can by my own understanding or effort block the Holy Spirit, but if I have faith, it is a gift.

So "the Holy Spirit has called me through the Gospel." We are back to the central Lutheran notion that the gospel is the way the word of God comes to us. But it remains a dead word on a page, or dead sound waves in a church, unless the Holy Spirit intervenes and acts, as we always pray this Spirit does, and as we always praise when this Spirit has called us. So the Holy Spirit "enlightens" us, makes us holy, keeps us in faith. We can talk about holiness later; two grand themes remain: the church and forgiveness.

God through the Holy Spirit "fully forgives my sins and the sins of all believers." Yesterday dare not haunt us, nor tomorrow. We are forgiven today, raised from the dead, given eternal life, as we return to our Baptism, repenting of our sins.

The Christian church? Here we say that the Holy Spirit "calls, gathers, enlightens, and sanctifies the whole Christian church on earth, and keeps it united with Jesus Christ in the one true faith."

This is a great ecumenical passage. If we often speak of Lutheranism on these pages, it is not in order to be sectarian but to be distinctive. It is false, say Lutherans, to think that the Holy Spirit calls and enlightens and sanctifies and keeps only them. They are part of the whole church. They are partners under the Holy Spirit with Roman Catholics and Baptists, with Japanese and Indian Christians who are not Lutheran.

They may not foresee the day when all the boundaries between churches come down. That kind of activity remains the work of the Holy Spirit to produce while through our "understanding and effort" we recognize the signals and achievements of it. Lutherans have learned to repent of the ways they have stood apart, and are careful not to misrepresent or downgrade other parts of the Christian church. As they hope ever more to converge in action and thought, they are most concerned that they and all Christians be faithful where they are. If they are faithful, it is to the credit of the Holy Spirit.

SUMMARY AND REFLECTION

"Do I have to believe *that?*" was the suspicious question with which we began. We wanted to do justice to the wary sense people have about doctrines and dogmas that churches add to the Scripture or use to say who's in, who's out, who's Christian, and who's not.

Instead, we saw that once we ask, "Do I *get* to believe that?" everything appears differently. Lutherans maintain that belief through the creeds and their statements is not an achievement, nor is it something pushed upon anyone. Rather, they think that the gospel is a gift which brings faith in what the creed points to.

Maybe we should compare the Bible and the Creed to the genetic programming of humans. Our genetic makeup is the original package that tells who and what we are and something of what we can become. Much happens to us after that package of DNA and cells is put together and we are born into the world. We come into contact with others. We relate to an environment. We have good and bad experiences. We develop this trait and neglect that one.

So it is with the church, which is often called the body of Christ, of which he is the head. The gospel of Jesus Christ as witnessed to in the Bible and the short statements like the Creed are the original programming. It determines that we are this and not that. Ours is not the Buddha story, nor the Marx story. We are something and so not something else. Yet given the gift of the Word and the Creed, we are then free to become. The church has different colors and a different character in various times and places. What shape it takes tomorrow, says the Lutheran Christian, will depend upon what each of us grasps when we say that God has made and preserves *me;* that Jesus Christ has redeemed *me:* that the Holy Spirit calls *me.* I am not the whole story, but the whole story can be mine. Now I can develop and grow.

1. What does it mean to you that the creeds are a gift?

2. What language for God means the most to you? Why?

3. What does it mean to you that you are a saint and a sinner?

4. What difference does the Apostles' Creed make for your faith?

5. What is the main question or idea that remains with you at the end of this session?

5
Faith and Daily Living

THE CRITICAL QUESTION

How are we to live?

This is a good question for inquirers and veterans alike.

Inquirers have good reason to ask it. They wonder what the Lutheran church expects of them. They know that every religious group, every Christian group, has certain expectations. Do this. Don't do that. They have heard, for example, about *cults*. Cults are very intense. They ask their members, often young people, to leave home and parents behind. They ask them to acknowledge a master, a head of the family. They have their members live together in communes or cells.

Then come the regulations. They address every detail of daily living. They prescribe whether or not cult members can eat meat or drink wine, and when they can eat and drink. They say who can have sex with whom, and on what terms, or whether no one can have sex with anyone. There are rules that command the followers to be in the streets selling flowers, or back in the camp sending out mailings. The members, in other words, turn over the powers of mind and conscience to a leader and to the group and its laws.

How terrible?

How satisfying!

One of the strong appeals of every intense religious group is its list of demands. Freedom strikes many people as terrible. It is a good deal easier to know how to live when someone spells out all the details. Every time people make a decision for themselves they spend energy. Are they doing the right thing? Are they pleasing God? Are they doing enough to stay in the group?

The inquirer at a mainstream Christian church has a good idea that nothing like this will be expected. Look around you in an inquirers' class and then in the church service. Odds are that the people going past the building, those asking about what goes on there, and the people who've been there a long time, look pretty much alike. If you follow members of some Christian groups around you will find that they have pretty specific demands. And some of the fastest-growing churches have the strictest demands. Lessening the demands might at first sound like a way to make churches more attractive, but it will not necessarily produce the fastest-growing churches. The strict ones grow. People *like* the law in religious life. What about the Lutherans? Where is their little manual? If you enroll on the campus of a church-related college, you expect the student manual to go into more detail about the moral life than if you go to a state university where there is *pluralism,* people of many moral patterns converging. If you "enroll" at a church, there must likewise be a manual of rules and regulations. If you pass a grade, you go on to a higher grade. You get recognition, and perhaps new roles and titles. You get closer to God. You are likely to win God's favor, likely to "be saved."

How satisfying?

How terrible!

Terrible, says the Lutheran church, because even if you follow all the laws, please all the leaders, impress all those who know you, you still have not begun to follow, please, and impress God. In fact, the more you know what God expects of you, the more you know the law of God, the worse off you'll be.

In fact, you'll despair.

And that is exactly where the Lutheran church thinks people should be if they want to learn how we are to live and what the good life with God is. This church has no interest in warping people's outlook. It is not happy when its members are "down in the dumps" or lacking self-esteem. We are not talking about psychology. We are talking about what God discloses about our true condition.

Perhaps a vivid image will make the point. In one of the liturgies of the Anglican church, people use the phrase "miserable offenders" to speak about themselves. "Offenders" makes them sound like criminals, and "miserable" makes them sound psychologically distressed. Yet, they use these words to confess their sins, and they don't *look* miserable. Watch the Lutherans doing something similar at Sunday worship. They may not look like criminal offenders. They probably won't look miserable. They are in church because they want to be, and not because they want to feel miserable. How can we explain this?

Let's use another image. People are riding on two trains rapidly speeding toward each other on a single track. Somehow, somewhere, a signal has been missed. The passengers, unaware, do what they have been doing. They may be dozing in serenity and security, thinking that this is the safest way to travel! They may be in the bar car, having a rousing time, or in the dining car, eating pretty good food. They are with friends, spouses or children, or they are smiling because they soon will meet them. But they are all miserable. If no one does anything, in seconds they will all be injured or dead. That is miserable.

Lutherans believe that, when it comes to rules and regulations in our relationship with God, we are in just this situation. The rules can lead us to doze, or to feel serene and secure. Having followed them, we can lean back, and claim that the rules weren't all *that* hard to follow. Or the rules can let us enjoy ourselves. Having heard them and having decided to obey them, we can figure that we might as well eat and drink, because we have taken care of God for another week. We're on our way safely, we can think.

But no, we're not on our way safely. We're in miserable condition. Someone has to act. Someone has to brake the trains or throw a switch, to change our fundamental condition. The Christian faith, the Bible, the Lutheran church have ways of addressing our misery. They point out ways to live which can minimize and, in some ways, remove the misery. If we learn something of this plot we can begin to answer the serious question, How are we to live?

THE PRESENTATION

The Christian faith and the Lutheran church are morally serious. It could not be otherwise. They want to be responsive to the God who calls them to be perfect even as God is perfect. They stand in awe of God as the Holy One. They cannot picture God being half-serious about divine law. They also know that the message of grace makes no sense except against the background of moral seriousness. Forget this, and you mess up the Lutheran understanding of faith.

Some Lutheran leaders complain that plenty of messing up goes on. One of them has gone around listening to Lutheran preaching. Everywhere he goes, he says, he hears preachers making the gospel clear to people. They do this against the background of attacks on legalism. They are against *works-righteousness,* which was Luther's word for the attempt to please God through works, through human efforts, through keeping the law. The sermons, this leader says, have phrases like this: "Don't try to please God by keeping the law! Don't try to impress God by being righteous! Don't try to merit salvation! Don't try to earn heaven!" Then the church visitor looks around and sees cozy and comfortable people leaning back with smiles, and asks, "Who's trying?"

A modern poet, W. H. Auden, wrote a Christmas piece called "For the Time Being" in which he described King Herod, ruler at the time of Jesus' birth, as worried. Why? Because Herod has been told that Jesus came to forgive sins, and to be gracious. This worries Herod. He can picture that the day will come in which many will say: "I like to commit sins; God likes to forgive them. Really, the world is admirably arranged!"

It can be like this, and it often is. People have to be trying before they can appreciate the gift of what Jesus Christ achieved for them. They have to know that while they like to commit sins, God cannot tolerate their sinning, or enjoy their sinning, or be easy on sinning. But Lutherans are also concerned about another way for their message to get messed up. They are concerned about *legalism.* Legalism has appeared often enough on Lutheran soil. It is easy for people to get together in the name of moral seriousness and then feel smug. They set standards and claim to keep them, and then impose them on others. They make long lists of what it is to be a good church member or follower of God, and then enforce what is on the list. Along the way, freedom goes out the window. So do joy in the gospel, spontaneous living, generosity of spirit, and true love.

It looks as if Lutheranism is on a tightrope between the *cheap grace* that does not take God seriously, and the legalism that does not take God's gospel seriously. A tightrope is not a comfortable place, however, so let's come down to earth with a good look at just what is expected of us—how we are to live.

The Lutheran understanding of God, Word, and Bible divides the message into *law* and *gospel*. In simplest terms, *law* represents the demands of God, and *gospel* is the promises of God.

Lutheran Christians agree about the gospel. They relish it as the means by which God is present among us with promise. Through the gospel, and not through works-righteousness, we are made right with God. Through the gospel, all the benefits that come with Jesus are ours. We live by the power of the gospel, for the love of Christ controls us when we walk in it. When God looks at us through the spectacles of the gospel, God sees not us in our sins but us identified with Christ.

The law is a different matter. It is harder to sort out. Some of the Lutheran creeds say that the only function of the law is to accuse the sinner and make things worse. We might feel we are keeping the law by not overtly stealing someone else's property, committing flagrant adultery, or just plain killing. Then we read the law and learn that even to *covet*—to think or wish that my neighbor's goods should be mine, or even to desire or hate or lust—keeps us from pleasing a holy God. Such thoughts and emotions are hard, if not impossible, for us to control. If they keep us from pleasing God, it makes it all worse. Defeat looms; despair sets in.

Lutheran Christians cannot say enough about the terrors of the divine law which accuses, especially when anyone is trying to please God. Martin Luther expressed this in a shocking way. In his lectures on the apostle Paul's letter to the Galatians, he mentioned that "sin, death, and the devil" are enemies of people who are trying to earn salvation. And he said one more thing: the law of God is also one of the enemies of those who aspire to salvation. But Luther's friends thought this statement too strong to print. How could the law of God be an enemy along with "sin, death, and the devil?" It could, and is, according to Paul in the Bible.

If that's the case, maybe Auden's Herod foresaw rightly, and cheap grace is in. Get rid of the law of God and live by the gospel of forgiveness only! The problem is, chaos would result. Another problem is, the Bible won't allow cheap grace; nor does Luther in his comments on the Bible.

Let's consider an important distinction, one that a Swedish Lutheran bishop named Gustav Aulen spelled out better than almost anyone else. Aulen agrees completely that when we speak of being saved, of being made right with God, *then* God's law always accuses and makes things worse. Then God's law leads the sinner, not to do good works, but to be more miserable and helpless. However, when we are not speaking directly of salvation, *then* God's law has a different function. If the gospel is "the power of God unto salvation," as Paul puts in, then the law, too, is a version of the "power of God unto . . . ." Unto what? Unto the care of the neighbor, the care of the earth, the care of society. Then we cannot say enough about how good things can be if we follow the law. It is, after all, or *before* all, God's law. God gave it as part of creation, as part of God's divine care, with good purposes in view.

The Ten Commandments are a decisive statement of the law. Let's see what they are about and what part they play in Christian life.

THE STUDY

The Ten Commandments have a good name in our society. Some people think they should be on classroom walls in the public schools. Then somehow, almost magically, morality would be beamed into the lives of children. They would fear God, respect parents and teachers, love each other, and be moral. These people wonder why the Supreme Court won't allow for the posting of these Commandments in classrooms. After all, they are part of our culture.

The problem is, the Ten Commandments don't just tell people not to kill and steal. They begin with the command to have no other god before God. This command is specific religion, which is unconstitutional on classroom walls.

The Ten Commandments are part of our culture. Everyone knows them. Well, not quite everyone. According to the Gallup Poll, everyone is *for* the Ten Commandments, but only a small minority of Americans can recite more than two or three of them. One thing an inquirer's class ought to do is at least confront the Ten Commandments.

In Luther's Small Catechism, a kind of textbook for old and young alike, the law, the Ten Commandments, is not a topic sneaked in at the back or in a footnote. The Ten Commandments comes first in the Catechism, taking up six of the 30 pages. In the Large Catechism it takes Luther almost fifty pages to get past the Ten Commandments, if it could be said he ever gets past them. This says that for Luther, and for Lutherans, the Ten Commandments count.

According to the Hebrew Scriptures, the Ten Commandments, or *Decalog,* is the law given by Yahweh to Moses for the people of Israel. From art, movies, cartoons, and Bible stories, people have an image of Moses carrying down from Mount Sinai two tables of stone on which these commandments were carved. The people of Israel cherished them. Jesus took these two tables and summarized them as two commands, to love God and to love the neighbor. He intensified them in his Sermon on the Mount. Jesus said that the condition of the heart is so important a person could not keep the commandments just externally. Of course, a person should not kill. But "I say unto you," Jesus said, that even those who merely hate their brother or sister are murderers and have not eternal life in him.

Clearly, this is the emphatic law of God. It allows for no compromise. It does not permit us to think of it half-seriously. What do we do with this powerful command of God to care for the neighbor, and for the earth? It does have something to say about how we are to live.

Inquirers who study the comments on the Commandments in the Small Catechism will notice the care Luther gives to them. In each case he helps us ask what a command means. In nine of the ten cases he tells us it means that we should "fear and love God so that" we do not do so-and-so. In the first case, "You shall have no other gods" he adds the word *trust* to his explanation: "We are to fear, love, and trust God above anything else." Fear and love. *Fear* here is not the emotion that paralyzes, but the sense of awe one has before the holy. Luther claims that the motivation for not doing badly and for doing good, must, however, include not just the fear of God but the love of God.

Three commands make up the *first table*. (Different methods of numbering the Commandments occur within Judeo-Christian tradition. For example, some people say it is the Seventh Commandment that forbids adultery, while in the Catechism it is Sixth. This results from the use of different but parallel texts in the Bible. So if we ask, "Who's right?" we can answer, "Both are.")

INTRODUCTION
I am the Lord your God.

THE FIRST COMMANDMENT
You shall have no other gods.

What does this mean for us?
We are to fear, love, and trust God above anything else.

THE SECOND COMMANDMENT
You shall not take the name of the Lord your God in vain.

What does this mean for us?
We are to fear and love God
so that we do not use his name
    superstitiously, or use it
to curse, swear, lie, or deceive,
but call on him in prayer, praise, and
    thanksgiving.

THE THIRD COMMANDMENT
Remember the Sabbath day, to keep it holy.

What does this mean for us?
We are to fear and love God
so that we do not neglect his Word
    and the preaching of it,
but regard it as holy
and gladly hear and learn it.

These first three commands speak of having no other gods, not taking the Lord's name in vain, and remembering the Sabbath day. What's at stake? Here God is disclosed as the One who is to be first and have first place. This is not to assure that God's selfish ego will be served. It is to assure that human purposes be best realized. Whenever we make gods of our money, nation, sex, success, or whatever, we are enslaved. Service of God is perfect freedom. The command against idols, then, is liberating.

To take the name of God in vain cheapens our speech and keeps us from being taken seriously. By keeping God's name holy, we show that speech is a divine gift which we are not lightly to misuse, or to misuse at all. To "curse, swear, lie, or deceive" in God's name is to ruin all chance to care for our neighbor through our speech. Instead, we are to use speech to call on God in "prayer, praise, and thanksgiving."

Then we will be showing care also for our neighbor through our speech.

The Sabbath reflects the seventh day on which God rested in the Genesis stories. We are to "keep it holy." Most Christians—Seventh-Day Adventists and some Baptists are rare exceptions—have chosen to keep the Sabbath on Sunday. This day is their weekly anniversary of Christ's resurrection. They follow New Testament words that say we are not to be judged by which holy days we keep, and find Sunday appropriate for their meal with the risen Lord. What they find important is the keeping of a day, setting it aside as holy. In the Catechism this means that we do not neglect the Word nor the preaching of it, but "gladly hear and learn it." And so we gather in a holy place to let God be present and heard among us, while we respond.

The second table spells out what makes for good human relations. It says, "We are to fear and love God so that we . . ." and then it spells out various comments on the commands. One command tells us to honor father and mother. This

THE FOURTH COMMANDMENT
Honor your father and your mother.

What does this mean for us?
We are to fear and love God
so that we do not despise or anger our
  parents and others in authority,
but respect, obey, love, and serve them.

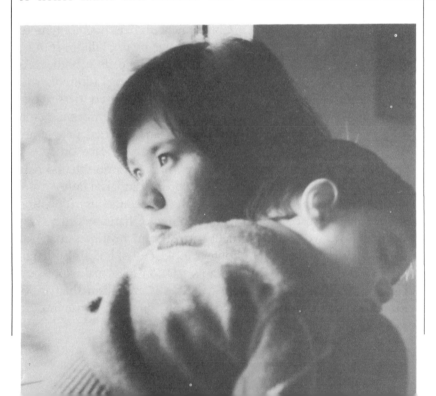

gets extended to "others in authority." Lutherans use it as a basis of respect for civil authority. We are to "respect, obey, love, and serve" civil leaders. Maybe we should not push inquirers too hard here! You may have in mind politicians who might have to be obeyed and served because they make the laws and have the power, but they seem hardly to merit respect and we cannot love them. We can joke about such things, and be highly diverse in our political opinions. But what is at stake is that authority also be seen as a way in which God acts among us. To despise it is to invite anarchy, a state of chaos in which God's care can hardly reach us. Lutherans use the Fourth Commandment (along with the First Article of the Creed) as a base for supporting the institutions of human life, the legitimate order that preserves and extends life.

THE FIFTH COMMANDMENT
You shall not kill.

What does this mean for us?
We are to fear and love God
so that we do not hurt our neighbor in any way,
but help him in all his physical needs.

THE SIXTH COMMANDMENT
You shall not commit adultery.

What does this mean for us?
We are to fear and love God
so that in matters of sex our words and conduct are pure and honorable,
and husband and wife love and respect each other.

"You shall not kill." Here we follow the Sermon on the Mount and are not to "hurt our neighbor in any way," which also means not hating. Then we turn this over positively and on the basis of this Commandment we are to help our neighbors in all their physical needs. The Lutheran movement in the Christian church is not content to keep life alive by not killing. It must participate in the care of bodies. As for not committing adultery, this means that "in matters of sex our words and conduct are pure and honorable" and married people are to "love and respect each other."

This Sixth Commandment receives more attention than others when people talk about moral conditions. Scandals against it are lurid. They keep the press and television news staffs busy. We often find people measured more by this command than any other. It is true that how we handle sexuality, trust, and promises made to others tells a great deal about how we look at all of life. In Lutheran understandings, there is a warm appreciation of sexual expression in marriage. There is less interest in crabby moralism than in legitimate expression of bodily and relational life—all in the interest of care of the neighbor.

"You shall not steal" means you are not to take property. But, again, there is a positive twist: you are to help neighbors "improve and protect" their "property and means of making a living." It may seem hard to do this in a competitive society like ours, where we often do in others so that we can advance. Yet the comment is clear: not stealing means more than not stealing. Care of the neighbor means acting positively towards the neighbor's property. Similarly, we are not merely to refrain from betraying, slandering, or lying about our neighbor. The turn comes again: you must defend neighbors, speak well of them, and explain their actions in the kindest way. It would be quite a change in our backbiting world if we were to treat others this way. We would be showing true care of the neighbor.

The next two Commandments (condensed into one in some lists) ask us not even to covet our neighbors' goods or spouse. We are to help them keep what is theirs, and teach fidelity to others. That is care. And those are the Commandments. Love God. Love the neighbor.

Now let's take a backward glance: what has this exercise been all about? It could be a waste of time learning the Commandments if Christians are not to be saved by doing the law. Now it is startling to read Luther in praise: "This much is certain: anyone who knows the Ten Commandments perfectly knows

THE SEVENTH COMMANDMENT
You shall not steal.

What does this mean for us?
We are to fear and love God
so that we do not take our neighbor's
    money or property,
or get them in any dishonest way,
but help him to improve and protect
his property and means of making a living.

THE EIGHTH COMMANDMENT
You shall not bear false
witness against your
neighbor.

What does this mean for us?
We are to fear and love God
so that we do not betray, slander,
    or lie about our neighbor,
but defend him, speak well of him,
and explain his actions in the kindest way.

THE NINTH COMMANDMENT
You shall not covet your
neighbor's house.

What does this mean for us?
We are to fear and love God
so that we do not desire to get our
    neighbor's possessions by scheming,
or by pretending to have a right to them,
but always help him keep what is his.

THE TENTH COMMANDMENT
You shall not covet your
neighbor's wife, or his
manservant, or his maid-
servant, or his cattle,
or anything that is your
neighbor's.

What does this mean for us?
We are to fear and love God
so that we do not tempt or coax away
    from our neighbor his wife or his
    workers,
but encourage them to remain loyal.

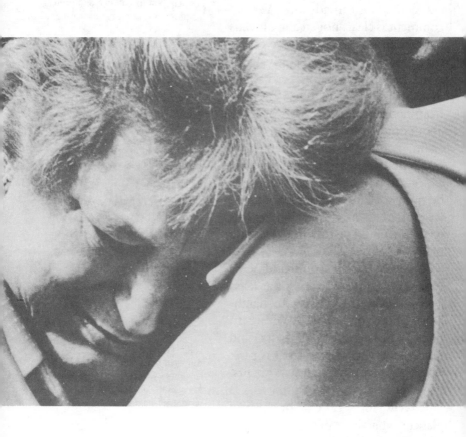

the entire Scriptures. In all affairs and circumstances [that person] can counsel, help, comfort, judge, and make decisions in both spiritual and temporal matters." This sounds like an exaggeration, and in a way it is. You have to catch on to how Luther speaks and writes: he loves to state an extreme position in order to get us to think. This extreme position happens to be true. The key is in the word *knows* as it relates to the Ten Commandments.

According to Luther's way of thinking, the Ten Commandments have to do with every aspect of every moral decision in life. To know them would be to have absorbed them thoroughly, and learned to observe them all. This, we know, cannot be done. But we have learned from them how God discloses a care for the ordering of life, for the things of the world, for the neighbor. What's left is the matter of motivation.

Why should a person know and follow the Commandments? How does anything good occur? On one level, we can say that you do not have to be a believer in order to do good. Lutherans do not believe you have to be Christian in order to uphold the law or serve the ways of God. Indeed, Lutherans believe that non-Christians often shame Christians by the way they thus serve God. Christians have no monopoly on justice. Good things can happen in nations which have been hardly touched by the Bible or Christian missionaries. (Here Lutherans differ from those Christians who believe that they must elect only their type of fellow Christians to office, or see their nation as Christian and many others as pagan.) Lutherans know that those who may not be "right with God," or "righteous before God," "made just," or "forgiven in Christ," may do right. They believe that *something* of the law of God is written on the heart. It belongs to the nature of things. It is part of the way things are. We can deduce this by reason. The law of God in the Bible shows us the source of the demands to do good and the good. It clarifies. It promotes the full seriousness of the moral claim.

Inquirers on Lutheran soil learn that they are to do good works, but the timing is all-important. They are not to do them before they are made righteous by God, in order to draw God's attention and favor. The problem with such an effort is that no matter how much they would do, it would never be enough. The further they got in the moral quest, the better they would get at finding out how far they have to go. They would be insecure, and finally, despairing. Instead, the good ways are to follow and to grow out of God's act to make them right and just and forgiven.

Now it can be seen that the whole Christian life becomes a life controlled by the love of Christ. Now the gospel comes into play. Now we get to be "as Christ" or "a Christ" to our neighbor. Whatever God does through Christ for the care of the neighbor, God now entrusts to us to carry on. We cannot rescue others; we are not perfect or innocent in our love and care. Jesus Christ was and is, so he stood in our place. For now he is to live in our actions and we are to be channels of his love. That is how we are to live.

SUMMARY AND REFLECTION

United Methodist theologian Albert Outler spent years studying the Christian past. He enjoyed preaching also and stayed close to congregations. He was once asked what he had learned through all his years about the gospel and the people. He had an emphatic answer. "All through the years I always thought I should preach, You've got to love! Then it suddenly hit me. The gospel announces, You *get* to love!"

This is the point of God's action among us. We get to love. We get to care. Instead of remaining self-seeking and self-centered beings, we are liberated. Through the Holy Spirit, Christ comes into our hearts. We begin to see the world in a new light. We see Christ in the acts of love done in His name. We see Christ in the needs of the sick, the imprisoned, the lonely, the hungry, as he said we would and should (Matthew 25). We are not paralyzed by our need to make ourselves just and right before God. We are not busy winning merit badges and Brownie points and silver stars or awards. We are free to see the cross of Christ as power for love and to act by that power.

For Jesus, that love makes one special demand. You've got to forgive. His parables show that this is the case. No, Outler would say, "You *get* to forgive." This means that our fundamental relation to others is not one in which we have to be petty, keep scorecards, wait for chances to even the score, or bear resentment for real or imagined hurts. Rather, we are to live in such a way that we and others can say that though there is sorrow for disturbed relationships and bad actions, there is room for a new start. Then we forgive.

A nineteenth-century Christian named Soren Kierkegaard once said that it was not hard for God to create a universe out of nothing. That was nothing. He started from nothing, so there was nothing there to offend holiness. But it is a very different thing for God to create a forgiven sinner. There God has to confront unholiness, all that violates the perfect. Yet God does forgive. God looks at the sinner "in Christ" and sees Christ's innocence, holiness, and perfection. On that basis we get a new start each day. Yesterday's guilt is gone; there is no worry about tomorrow. What's more, we get to pass it on. We are to be forgiven and to forgive, to wipe slates clean, to have new starts. Through this act, Christ is served, Christ is present, and we are free.

1. What does God's law mean to you? God's gospel?

2. What does it mean to you that you are a "miserable offender"?

3. What does it mean to you that "you get to love"?

4. How do you respond to the question, How are we to live?

5. What is the main idea or question that remains with you at the end of this session?

6
Spiritual Growth

THE CRITICAL QUESTION

How shall we pray?

First, the answer: We are to pray in trust.

Now, more about the question. How shall we pray? is one of the most natural things for inquirers to inquire about. The disciples of Jesus had it high on their priority list. "Teach us to pray!" they asked Jesus. Students of world religions say that at the heart of every religion is the need for its participants to feel they are or can be in contact with a divine power. Otherwise, why make the claim that a divine being exists? Or what should be done about the claims such beings make on people?

Prayer is "in." When Americans are taken hostage, and then interviewed, almost all of them say boldly that they have prayed as never before. If they are rescued, they say that their rescue was in answer to prayer. Or they were rescued because they prayed, or because God singled them out and answered their prayers. If someone is not rescued, their loved ones still say they prayed, but their prayer was not answered. They ask the public to remember them in prayer. "There are no atheists in foxholes," is another saying about people's tendency to pray in life-and-death situations.

Prayer seems to be an instinct of the human heart. It is hard to suppress prayer in times of great joy or terror. Sometimes prayer seems to be favored more than God: people talk more about prayer than about God, whom they may conceive as "the One Upstairs" or in some other vague terms.

If you listen closely, you will hear that prayer tells a great deal about how people conceive God and church and faith. Some people seem to think of God as a magic being whom they can invoke from time to time. Some picture God like a watch in their pocket they consult on occasion, but like the watch, God never gets in the way—both act at the convenience of the owner. Still others think God is too remote to hear and too powerless to act. If we listen to Lutherans talking about prayer, we will learn much about how they conceive of God and our relations with God.

THE PRESENTATION

How shall we pray?

What do we expect in the language of prayer? Some feel that the only, and best, Christian prayer is one of resignation: "If it be your will . . . ." Of course, we are to pray to conform to God's will. The night before he is put to death, Jesus prays, "Not my will, but thine, be done. . . ." The problem with prayers of resignation is that people who pray them can soon expect too little. Or they can sound like defeatists who don't ever expect to get their way.

Professor Donald Capps of Princeton Theological Seminary has a better image for prayer. It voices well the Lutheran tradition of prayer. We do not expect to have our will and way all the time. Nor do we resign ourselves to God's mysterious will, which seems rarely to match our desires. Instead, Capps urges that we think of prayer as a mode of communication between two who know each other well. They build up expectations for each other. They develop familiarity. And then they are open to surprises in one another. My spouse may ask for the Taj Mahal "if it be my will," and it might be my way, but my spouse ought to know about the limited supply of Taj Mahals, and my limited means. A child may ask to be taken to the circus, knowing that the answer will probably be yes; this is a reasonable expectation of a parent who cares and with whom the child communicates. And surprise! Not only that, we'll go for a week to Disney World, and then see the coral reefs, and the Everglades and . . . .

Some people in the late stages of a terminal disease pray for a "Taj Mahal." They pray for an arrest of malignant cells. They pray for a reversal of the deteriorative process that has taken vital organs. They pray to be exempted from death. They will not get it (though who can limit the "miracles" people may legitimately pray for?). Yet if they trust God they will get something else. They will get what

Romans 8:38-39 promises: that God will see to it that love is stronger than death; that nothing, including death, shall separate them from the love of God in Christ. Someone who has talked both in awe and familiarity with God knows such trust and builds on such trust. A 5'4" adult with a thin voice may pray to become younger, a basketball center, and a Metropolitan Opera Star, and then add, "nevertheless not my will, but thine, be done," and achieve none of these things. But if this person trusts God, he or she can live knowing that God is daily using the gifts he or she does possess, and will use them long after the center has been replaced on the team, long after the Met Star's own voice failed.

What matters in our relationship with God is developing this intimacy, this trust. What matters is this pattern of communication, expectation, and the gift of surprise. Most people call this *prayer,* or *the life of prayer.* Some speak of it as *spirituality,* for we find in prayer a kind of communion in spirit with God the Holy Spirit. Whatever else religion may be—doing good in the world, giving gifts, praising God—this spiritual life needs care. Out of it comes nurture and closeness to God.

Lutherans pray a good deal, even if not always as spontaneously as some other Christians. They refuse to get into arguments over the proper form. People may grow suspicious if believers cannot put into their own words their thoughts in conversation with God. And certainly God does not need human eloquence to answer prayer. But impromptu prayer is not the only effective style. Nor is it more heartfelt, or more compelling. Anyone who has suffered through long, rambling prayers in divine worship may wonder whether even God is not growing bored by such a casual recital. More formal prayer has its place.

Intercessory prayer in the congregation is the most characteristic prayer among Lutherans. It is the prayer they pray just before Holy Communion or at a climactic point in other services. Lutherans think of intercessory prayer as urgent and generous. It is loving one's neighbor on one's knees. It gives expression to the fact that all believers are priests, that all can approach God and pray for this person in military service, this college student, this unemployed fellow member, this sufferer, this family of the deceased, this couple on their wedding anniversary. Do people pray, "Not our will, but thine, be done?" No, they pray, "We have often talked to you, God, and because we love you and wait upon you expectantly we are bold to say that . . . ." Then they commend the person to God's love which outlasts separation, illness, and even death.

Lutherans are encouraged to pray when they rise and retire, before and sometimes after meals. They often set aside special times for prayer. It would be hard to find a distinctive ritual or routine that they use. Prayer is very ecumenical, and Lutherans learn from the spiritual life of others—Roman Catholic, Baptist, Mennonite— just as they hope to contribute to others' spiritual lives. Lutherans hold several special attitudes about prayer which we will consider.

First, Lutherans are somewhat uneasy with mysticism. Mysticism is a popular subject these days. The mystic, who used to dwell in the desert or the monastery cell, but can appear in any quiet place, seeks a unity with what we may call the All, the One, the Universe, God. Mystics try to get out of themselves. In fact, *ecstasy,* which is a part of mysticism, means precisely that. Mystics try to be *enthusiastic,* which literally means filled with or possessed by the divine. The apostle Paul sometimes talks in terms that let people regard him as a mystic. Certainly not every aspect of mysticism is out of bounds for Lutherans. There have been Lutheran mystics, and you, too, may experience your spirit rising above the normal bounds of practical life to be close to God.

This is not forbidden to Lutherans, but they are somewhat uneasy about it. There is one particular aspect of mysticism that makes Lutheran Christians nervous. Mystical language often implies a kind of union with God on God's level. It implies a sort of achievement, as climbing by degrees to God's favor and to intimacy with God. Such mysticism easily translates to something like the moral achievement believers thought they needed in order to impress God and be saved. It is something like the use of reason that led theologians to think they could contemplate their way to good terms with God.

The Reformation criticized such approaches, which kept people so busy they could not understand or relish the gospel. It is as if these people were sawing away at the cell bars of the jail that kept them imprisoned in sin and self, when all along Christ was trying to get their attention to show them that the key had been turned, the lock was undone, and the door was open for walking through.

In the life of mysticism and prayer, Lutherans stress that people seek union with God on the human level. God is accessible to us precisely because God has revisited this world and remains present in it in the person Jesus Christ. We pray in the name of Jesus Christ, because through him we have open access to God who stoops or condescends to be reached through Christ. John 1:14 says that God dwelt among us when the Word was made flesh, when Jesus brought the fulness of God to us.

Prayer, then, is not a climbing, a striving, or an achievement. It is the acceptance of a gift, a responding to a call, an enjoyment of a conversation. It becomes a way of life. Dietrich Bonhoeffer, who lost his life to the Nazis during World War II, liked to think of faith and trust as the *cantus firmus* of life. *Cantus firmus* refers to the chief melodic theme that runs through a musical composition. Once it is in place the *cantus firmus* can go almost unnoticed while other melodies of sweetness, drama, and excitement are woven around it. So it is with prayer. Prayer is the *cantus firmus,* the continuous, grounded, sometimes-taken-for-granted basis of life. Union with God not at God's level but at our human level is prayer as Lutherans speak of it.

The second distinctive attitude is not unique to Lutherans but it is Lutheran. It has to do with how we speak about the God who relates to us in prayer. Here the Lutheran way falls between two extremes. One set of believers is like the deists of two centuries ago. While theists believe in a personal God involved in human life, *deists* believe that there is a suprahuman, invisible, force or principle that stands behind the order and morality of the world. But, having set the world in motion, this divine-like power is neither personal nor involved in human life. Humans are on their own. Humans do not pray to such a god, unless prayer is considered only an act of self-improvement. Some of the founders of America were deists. They reverently referred to the Grand Architect, or Providence, or the Creator. But they did not refer to the God of Abraham and Sarah who was involved with Israel, or the One with whom Jesus spoke so intimately in his mountain and garden retreats.

There is an opposite extreme which is more tempting to Lutherans. It is a kind of *folk piety* which claims to know exactly what God is doing in detail all the time. It implies that the persons praying know exactly what God's will is.

Listen to how, when something bad happens like the murder or agonizing illness of a child, people will speak for God. Some will say that God caused the death or the agony. They might say it is God's will. Is God, then, the agent of evil? In response, Lutherans affirm that the child was not singled out for punishment. Jesus talked about people born blind, or struck by a falling tower, and these are not God's will. Falling towers happen to kill people who happen to be standing in the way of their fall. But, if God did not *cause* the evil, maybe God *allowed* it. Yet if God has the power to prevent evil and does not care to use it, thoughtful people will start comparing this God to the worst kind of human parents.

Lutherans who have studied the way Jesus Christ died are more ready to say that in Jesus' death, God took part in suffering. Lutherans don't sentimentalize God and make God a half-powerful figure with a handkerchief who cries a lot. Lutherans stress instead that God is deeply involved with human suffering. God suffers with and changes with the people in their circumstances. As one woman with a progressive illness wrote on the last page of her diary: "All I really pray for now is the tears of God." The Bible is full of pictures of a God with tears. This is the One we approach in prayer.

THE STUDY

Let's focus our attention again on our textbook, the Small Catechism, where Luther gives fresh meaning to the parts of the Lord's Prayer. It is the model prayer. Jesus prays it when the disciples ask him how to pray. In Christian communities, it is the most familiar, most prayed, and most used quotation from the whole Bible. Study of it helps us understand an approach to prayer, spirituality, the inner life, the journey, or whatever we call our response to grace.

In commenting on the Ten Commandments Luther asked each time, "What does this mean?" He addresses the same question to the seven separate prayers in the Lord's Prayer. There is also another question to be asked. Three times, Luther asks, "When does this [activity] happen?" Luther's short responses summarize the Lutheran understanding of the Lord's Prayer, and of all prayer.

Luther's introduction to prayer condenses what we have said so far about communication, intimacy, boldness, and trust: God encourages us to believe that "he is truly our Father and we are his children." Here we encounter male imagery for God with the word *Father*. It has an important point. It is a metaphor for the kind of relationship and communication that develops between children and good and trustworthy parents, between us and God. When we pray to God, we can talk with complete confidence, just as children would talk with loving parents.

"Hallowed be your name." Here we remind ourselves that God's name does not need help to be made holy, but we pray that *we* will change, and stand in awe of God. The Catechism claims that this happens best when we teach God's Word purely and live according to

THE INTRODUCTION
Our Father in heaven.

What does this mean?
Here God encourages us to believe
that he is truly our Father
and we are his children.
We therefore are to pray to him with
    complete confidence
just as children speak to their loving
    father.

THE FIRST PETITION
Hallowed be your name.

What does this mean?
God's name certainly is holy in itself,
but we ask in this prayer
that we may keep it holy.

When does this happen?
God's name is hallowed
whenever his Word is taught
in its truth and purity
and we as children of God live in
    harmony with it.
Help us to do this, heavenly Father!
But anyone who teaches or lives
    contrary to the Word of God
dishonors God's name among us.
Keep us from doing this, heavenly
    Father!

THE SECOND PETITION
Your kingdom come.

What does this mean?
God's kingdom comes indeed
without our praying for it,
but we ask in this prayer that it
    may come also to us.

When does this happen?
God's kingdom comes
when our heavenly Father gives us his
    Holy Spirit,
so that by his grace we believe his
    holy Word
and live a godly life on earth now
    and in heaven forever.

THE THIRD PETITION
Your will be done,
on earth as in heaven.

What does this mean?
The good and gracious will of God is
    surely done without our prayer,
but we ask in this prayer
that it may be done also among us.

When does this happen?
God's will is done when he hinders and
    defeats every evil scheme and purpose
of the devil, the world, and our sinful
    self,
which would prevent us from keeping his
    name holy
and would oppose the coming of his
    kingdom.
And his will is done
when he strengthens our faith
and keeps us firm in his Word as long as
    we live.
This is his gracious and good will.

it. So Lutheran prayer is connected with preaching, teaching, and living.

"Your kingdom come." Again, because God is always the agent, the kingdom comes no matter what. But, we pray that the kingdom comes "also to us." When does it come? When we receive the Spirit, believe the Word, and live a godly life now and forever. If you were not surprised to hear that answer, you are doing well as an inquirer. You are catching on to consistent and expectable answers. Note the Lutheran themes of gift, faith, and response. They grow out of the same glowing core, and are not arbitrary pearls on a string.

"Your will be done, on earth as in heaven." As always, God's will happens without our prayer. But we want it done "also among us." When does it happen? When God breaks the things that stand in the way of his will, and when he makes us strong in faith: that is God's will.

"Give us today our daily bread." This prayer sounds so simple and meager. It seems like such a small request. By the time the Catechism is done with it, however, it has become the whole catalog of human needs. We ask God to attend to them, not with worry about tomorrow, but just for this day. And we are to receive with thanks. A preacher once repeated the story about Jesus and the ten lepers. Jesus healed all of them. Only one returned to give thanks. That one, said the preacher, represents the church, the community which gives thanks for the blessings that everyone, including the sinful, receives. What is "bread" for Lutherans when they pray this prayer?

Luther writes, "Daily bread includes everything needed for this life, such as food and clothing, home and property, work and income, a devoted family, an orderly community, good government, favorable weather, peace and health, a good name, and true friends and neighbors." Bread includes everything. We are not to put limits around the subjects we can converse about with God.

"Forgive us our sins as we forgive those who sin against us." This is the heart, the core, the gospel of forgiveness. It commits us "on our part," to "heartily forgive and gladly do good to those who sin against us."

THE FOURTH PETITION
Give us today our daily bread.

What does this mean?
God gives daily bread, even without
    our prayer, to all people, though sinful,
but we ask in this prayer
that he will help us to realize this
and to receive our daily bread with
    thanks.

What is meant by "daily bread"?
Daily bread includes everything needed
    for this life,
such as food and clothing, home and
    property,
work and income, a devoted family,
an orderly community, good government,
favorable weather, peace and health,
a good name, and true friends and
    neighbors.

THE FIFTH PETITION
Forgive us our sins
as we forgive those
who sin against us.

What does this mean?
We ask in this prayer
that our Father in heaven would not hold
    our sins against us
and because of them refuse to hear our
    prayer.
And we pray that he would give us
    everything by grace,
for we sin every day
and deserve nothing but punishment.
So we on our part will heartily forgive
and gladly do good to those who sin
    against us.

THE SIXTH PETITION
Save us from the time of trial.

What does this mean?
God tempts no one to sin,
but we ask in this prayer that God would
    watch over us and keep us
so that the devil, the world, and our
    sinful self may not deceive us
and draw us into false belief, despair,
    and other great and shameful sins.
And we pray that even though we are
    so tempted
we may still win the final victory.

THE SEVENTH PETITION
And deliver us from evil.

What does this mean?
We ask in this inclusive prayer
that our heavenly Father would save us
    from every evil to body and soul,
and at our last hour would mercifully
    take us
from the troubles of this world to himself
    in heaven.

"Save us from the time of trial." Or, "Lead us not into temptation." Here the enemies of God—"the devil, the world, and our sinful self"—are seen as the deceivers. Christians do not believe temptation will disappear. Indeed, as you grow in faith and grace you become bigger, rising higher for a possibly greater fall. This prayer asks not that temptation disappear but that "we may still win the final victory."

"And deliver us from evil." Through the ages, people have been believers as much for this as for any reason. This is an "inclusive prayer" that applies to "every evil to body and soul." It can mean the terror of the feudal lord who could storm our hut in a drunken fury. It can mean famine and earthquake, separation and loneliness, fear, loss of courage or faith, abuse, rape, Alzheimer's disease, AIDS, laziness and failing grades, military defeat, nuclear war, misspent and misappropriated funds, injustice, or whatever. Deliverance from evil, in the life of prayer, also includes the hour of death and expects the love of God for the dying person to continue eternally.

And there is an "Amen." It means "Yes, it shall be so." Luther describes such prayers or petitions as "pleasing to our Father," who hears the prayers. Otherwise, why would God have commanded us to pray in this way, and promised to hear us?

In the Large Catechism there is more that explains a Lutheran way of prayer and spirituality. Surprisingly, Luther begins by reminding us that prayer is commanded. It is not an option, though its forms may be. Luther chides people who think it's all right to have someone else pray for them; then they do not follow the command to pray, and they fail to have the richest possible relationship with God.

Furthermore, Luther writes, mere repetition and length have nothing to do with prayer. "It is quite true that the kind of babbling and bellowing that used to pass for prayers in the church was not really prayer." It might be exercise, but it is not prayer. "To pray," Luther says, "is to call upon God in every need. This God requires of us; he has not left it to our choice."

While we *can* pray for others through intercessory prayer we do not expect saints, or Mary, or the departed to put in a word for us. We have no access to these deceased figures whom we admire and seek to follow. Instead, we have direct access, through Christ, to the Maker of all things. We may admire eloquent and passionate experts at prayer, but we do not need their prayers. As Luther writes, "The prayer I offer is just as precious, holy, and pleasing to God as those of St. Paul and the holiest of saints."

Prayer is, then, the really democratic act among all the things believers do. It has been pointed out that all the liturgical changes—that is, all the reforms of worship—which Jesus addresses, come down to one thing: the reform of prayer. Jesus does not address the nature of candles, incense, robes, service books, or organs, though he says nothing that would cause us to reject their use in worship. Rather Jesus addresses the issue of the poor having access to the Temple. Temple sacrifices cost. Even Joseph and Mary had to bring two turtle doves. But prayer, talking with God, costs nothing, Jesus says. No matter who you are, where you are, or what your talents and needs are, these teachings insist that you are equally commanded and free to appear before God in prayer.

SUMMARY AND REFLECTION

Inquirers into the Lutheran church sometimes express frustration. They are looking for mimeographed lists of rules and regulations and get nothing more than the Ten Commandments. And these come wrapped in a package which acknowledges that no one can really keep these rules and regulations. "The love of Christ," instead, "controls us," and we are quite free in our way of life.

Now comes another frustration. It would be so reassuring if an authority figure would gather us into a family and give us precise spiritual disciplines. Perhaps you have friends who go to yoga class and learn spiritual disciplines. They have exercises, postures, mind-clearing exercises. Or there are Buddhists who learn how to breathe, and stare, and create the Void. Or maybe you've heard "Hare Krishna," being chanted by youths who say the same thing hundreds of times, and who dance and wear robes and in general follow the guru and know exactly who they are and what they are to do. In contrast, we often are left on our own. We are encouraged to find our own hours and places, our own company and words, for prayer and spirituality.

Well, it is not quite *that* loose. There are times of day and specific activities that almost cry out to be addressed by prayer. There are always *eucharistic* prayers at the Lord's Supper. These are model prayers of thanks for all God does. Prayer also accompanies Baptism. Prayer is part of every gathered service of worship.

There are no needed props, since prayer can be the direct language of people. Yet many Lutherans will use the Psalms and other prayer-filled parts of the Bible. There have been great Lutheran people of prayer whose words have often helped us frame our thoughts and prayers. There are books called *Lutheran Book of Prayer* and *Lutheran Book of Worship*. However, we do well to set an atmosphere for attentive prayer. There are prayer desks and candles and plaques to serve as reminders. There are calendars with daily prayers on them. We are free to do all of them, commanded to do none of them, only to pray itself.

Should we meditate? The Bible commands meditation, and people value it. In some traditions, like Buddhism, meditation is designed to get people out of the story, as it were. People seek to "center" their consciousness, or to lose it, to get out of the stream of life and ideas and events. Such "centering" might be a useful step toward Christian meditation.

Christian meditation, however, does have a content. It derives *from* the story. It is not a means of achieving union with God and the All. It is a base for reflecting on the wonderful things God has done. It allows for pondering the puzzling things God does not seem to be doing. It permits agony over what one does not understand, but agony in the context of the One who hears, who suffers with us. Most of all, it permits a redirecting of life in light of the conversation with God. It permits a new resolve.

This resolve includes a concern to continue the life of prayer. While Christians in the Lutheran tradition do not consider themselves to be winning by achievement, they do picture growth in grace. They walk and talk more closely with God. This is the gift that grows out of our response to the command to pray, to develop the spiritual life, to undertake the inward journey in a world of external cares.

1. What is the role of prayer in your life now?

2. What role would you like prayer to have in your life?

3. What can you do to help nurture spiritual growth in prayer?

4. What is the main idea or question that remains with you at the end of this session?

7
Called and Nourished

THE CRITICAL QUESTION

What happens next?

This is the seventh and last session of this manual. It points to the end. This does not mean that your inquirer's class has to stop meeting, or that your questions as inquirers have all been answered. Some congregations like to hold further sessions about their own history and ways and expectations. Some inquirers want to explore more the meaning of the faith. They will find pastors and other congregational leaders very willing to meet privately and help them pursue the inquiry. But for our study of this manual, it is the end.

The end. When things come to an end, they press new beginnings on people. For instance, inquirers who have not previously done so will be making a decision. They will be asking, "How do I follow up on what I have studied here?" Many of them have inquired about a faith they have long known and shared: they wanted to deepen their knowledge. Or they came to a class because someone they cared about was coming. It is hoped they will now pass it on, by inviting others to this inviting church, whether to refresh their knowledge or to explore it for the first time.

Other inquirers knew all along that they were going to accept what was being taught by this pastor, this leader, this manual. Unless these seven sessions have created a new stumbling block, they will follow their intentions and become a part of the congregation. Still others who started with nothing more than curiosity and friendliness, will find themselves moved by the Holy Spirit to say yes. They want to be part of the body of Christ, of the whole Christian church, through this Lutheran church. What happens next? According to their circumstance and local custom, they will, upon their confession of faith, be "affirmed in their Baptism," "received into membership," "accepted upon profession of faith," or "restored." The term means less than the reality: that they will be fully *incorporated,* made a member of the local body. If it has not happened before, they first will be made a member of the body of Christ, through Baptism.

We should pause for a moment to consider a fourth kind of situation: the decision not to decide, or to decide against following through further. What happens to the inquirer who has patiently, perhaps prayerfully, followed this route for seven sessions and found herself or himself unable to say a wholehearted yes to what went on? The most important thing to say is that an inviting church will continue to care about you. It will not be pushy. It will not pressure you or look down on you or judge you. There is no point in having an inquiry unless it is free, unless it permits a variety of outcomes. You may remain a member of another Christian body, or you may choose a different one. This congregation will regard you as a full member of the body of Christ, and pray that you minister well and be well ministered to wherever you go in the Christian body. You may not find faith being worked in your heart, and therefore you cannot say an honest yes to questions about personal faith that are a part of joining the church. This congregation still does not turn its back or close its heart. We will pray for you and show continued concern for you, because we believe that trust in God, the gift of faith, the experience of grace, and the hope of eternal life with God, make all the difference in a person's destiny. Yet we cannot explain how and why faith happens to some honest inquirers and not to others. The church does not force conversion. It does not want to make hypocrites out of people by having them say yes when they mean no or maybe. It hopes you will think, "Someday." But this church does not worship a God who preys and pounces like a hunter stalking game—watching for you to be weak and off your guard, and then taking advantage of you. And if you never become a Christian, we can continue to respect and love you—as we hope all other Christians can.

THE PRESENTATION

What happens next?

Some of you may have thought that it's about time to move on. We've spent too many paragraphs and minutes on what is a commonsense item. Yet it is often true that the most taken-for-granted items need the most thoughtful attention. Some of us know what we want to do and what we might be asked to do, but others may not. It is good to have set out our expectations and covenants. We have just spelled out the options.

There is another reason for this little exercise. If you reread or rethink the lines, you will see that in all cases, some sort of decision has to occur. People in each situation must decide. Not to decide is also to decide. For instance, people who can put on the brakes or change the switching as two trains are coming toward a crash, and then do not, are making a decision—in this case, a decision for destruction and death. To decide is to respond to a call to faith and life. Not to decide is also to respond. And by posing this case of "what happens next" to an inquirer and a class, we have had a picture of an important element in Christian life.

Let's call it *response*. When Lutherans call for decision, they may not do it quite like some. It is easy for evangelists—who truly speak in the name of God, of Christ, of the Holy Spirit and who speak of the gift of faith and grace—to push so hard that they twist the faith. You can make deciding into one more achievement of busy people who are out to please God. You can place so much weight on the human will and intelligence that the human, not God, should be credited for achieving access to God, for meriting God's pleasure. If your will, your psychology, your striving, your busyness are stressed too much—then the gospel itself gets distorted.

It might be better to switch the term from *decide* to *respond*. In responding, we are still involved, but the essential signals and all the credit come from and go to God, who remains in loving care and in charge. Then we hear the voice of God calling, for God is the real inviter in an inviting church. God says, "I have made you for my own, and I beckon you to recognize this." It is to this invitation that you respond. You see the cross of Christ and recall the story of what happened in it. "Are you moved?" is the question. Are you moved by the fact that you helped put Jesus on the cross? Are you moved to welcome his gift, to become part of his resurrected life? You feel the power of the Holy Spirit calling. The word is: you may not feel acceptable, but you are accepted. You may have put up barriers against faith, but you can respond by letting them fall, so that the Holy Spirit can incorporate you into the body of Christ, and give you power to act in faith. God would work good in you; it does not depend on you, for if it did, you would always be insecure. You may ask, "Am I pleasing God?" Instead: it pleases God, through the Holy Spirit, to do the reaching out, the forgiving, the incorporating.

Now, when this call for response comes, you may well ask, "What happens next?" And one good answer is that you experience the call and the nurture through Baptism and the Lord's Supper. Recall that we began this inquiry, this tour of faith, with a tour of a church. We saw the Baptism font and the table for the Lord's Supper. We are back to the beginning. Baptism and the Lord's Supper are good pictures of the way God calls and nourishes and the way we respond. But Baptism and the Lord's Supper are not only pictures; they are themselves means of grace by which God does something in us and among us. Keep both ideas together: in these sacraments, picture and realize God's action.

Sacraments. We just used the word, and it is not one we use at the supermarket or in the legislature. It is one of those rare church terms. Many other church terms we share with the world: for example, people are "reconciled to God" in Jesus Christ and humans are "reconciled to each other" instead of being divorced. But *sacrament* is a word unique to the chruch. The word *sacrament* is not in the Bible. It is a useful term that people are free to define in different ways to describe a reality never quite found apart from the church. Rather than argue about how others besides Lutherans use it—and thus end up with more sacraments, or none at all!—we can serve best by saying what it is in the Lutheran church.

A sacrament to Lutherans means a sacred or holy act that God established. This means God commanded that it happen and connected a promise with it. While there are invisible means of being in touch with grace, a sacrament uses visible means like water, bread, and wine. One easy way to remember what the "visible means" are for Lutherans is to remember a blunt saying by a British clergyman, Martin Thornton. He once said that "all you need to express the physical side of Christian rites is a loaf of bread, a bottle of wine and a river." And, yes, since nothing magic occurs in Baptism and

the Lord's Supper, these visible means are connected with the Word of God, which is always what gives faith and achieves God's effects.

The Lutheran church makes much of the sacraments, both as pictures and as real means of grace. Some people coming to the Lutheran church from the "high" sacramental churches—the Roman Catholic, Eastern Orthodox, and Anglican Churches—will feel at home with this view, though they may find the usual expressions of the sacraments a bit simpler and less adorned than what they are used to. People coming from the "low" sacramental or nonsacramental churches may be a bit puzzled. Some believers, like the Quakers, do not have sacraments at all. They think that the sacraments, with their visible means, are temptations to idolatry. Or they maintain that the sacraments confuse the simplicity of faith. The Salvation Army, whose Christian devotion few would question, does not celebrate the Lord's Supper. But the vast majority of Christians are baptizers and communers. Many of them see the picture and reality of the sacraments to be less central than do Lutherans. And some might think the Lutheran view is a bit "high." They will see the reverence with which Lutherans baptize and commune as too formal an expression of simple faith. On the other hand, they will also see a wide range of Lutheran sacramental practices, some more simple, some more formal.

Lutherans consider humans to be ritual beings. Watch children at their games. Observe civic life. Think of your calendar of Thanksgiving Days and Christmases and family observances. These point to the fact that things "stick" best, or we give them our best devotion, when they are done in regularized ways. Yet, such psychology is not enough to justify the rites of Baptism and the Lord's Supper. Here as always we "let God be God," and make God's activity central. God being God is free to show love in any number of ways. The command to baptize followed God's choice to receive us, initiate us, make us God's own, wash away our sins through Baptism. So we joyfully respond, and baptize. The command to commune followed God's choice to be present among us, to forgive sins, to keep us in fellowship with Christ, to nurture us by the Holy Spirit when we gather in faith at a table and receive bread and wine. So we happily respond, and commune.

In these seven sessions we have always called this section of the session "The Presentation." We have presented something or other, and then moved on to study it. Now an extra meaning of *presenting* is becoming clear. We find that God presents God's self in Baptism. We talk about the "real presence" of Christ in the Lord's Supper; Christ comes in a special way to make real his promises and let us enjoy his company. These are presentations of faith and divine life. Let's study them.

THE STUDY

Let's take "what happens next" seriously. If you have not been baptized and want to respond in faith, now you will be baptized. It is obvious to anyone who has been to church regularly that Lutherans baptize infants. Not all Christians do. There are no clear biblical texts that say one should or should not baptize infants. Centuries of scholarship have not so far settled this. Some Christians say the New Testament defines Baptism in such a way that it takes an act of faith first, and that not-yet-reasonable and responsible infants cannot make that act. Other Christians say the New Testament would have named people it wanted excluded from Baptism; instead, the New Testament pictures whole households being baptized, which probably included youngest children.

Such ways of deducing what went on in the past are not very satisfying when we have questions for today. The question shifts: what do we picture going on that causes Lutherans to agree with most Christians, and baptize children? Let it be said that there are reasons for some uneasiness about the practice. There are some good things to say about believer's Baptism, as it is called by Baptists and others who insist on a reasoned and resolved act of faith before Baptism. People who "decide for Christ" and go through an agony of decision are probably more ready psychologically to accept a disciplined life than are many who were baptized as infants. An example can be found in European countries, where almost all children are baptized, but not many follow through. Yes, risks are there with infant Baptism, but we believe there are ways to face them.

Lutherans ask what Baptism of all ages sets out to picture and to realize. If you have followed the logic of Lutheranism in observing and celebrating the gospel you can see something special in Baptism. Here, as so often happens, an act of the church is a model of what all the acts of the church are about. Lutherans stress in Baptism that faith is a gift, not an achievement. The child is not achieving faith or Baptism. Instead, God is moving this child into a loving relation, putting a name on this child as on one adopted, making the child part of the covenant, incorporating him or her. In Baptism, Lutherans stress also that grace is free, a gift and not an achievement. The child, "born to a fallen humanity," is helpless about winning God's favor. A coo and a smile will not do. But the loving heart of God gives grace. Lutherans believe that Baptism pictures and realizes faith and grace as free gifts of God to people of all ages.

One other point needs to be made. Some insist that Baptism occurs only with *immersion*—that is, baptizing by submerging completely in water. Lutherans are not against immersion. They maintain an image of immersion in the Catechism, speaking of being "buried with Christ" by Baptism, and that we come up out of the water "risen with Christ." Yet they believe that as long as they use water, although in smaller amounts and in more convenient ways, they are fulfilling the command and getting the promises connected with baptismal faith. Enough about our differences: there is much we can learn from the Lutheran understandings of Baptism and the Lord's Supper.

Let's turn, again, to the Small Catechism, which in a few lines outlines it all. Baptism is "not water only"—that would be magic—but water "used together with God's Word and by his command." Now, Baptism is not only a picture of God's kind of action; it is *God in action*. Listen to Luther: "In Baptism God forgives sin, delivers from death and the devil, and gives everlasting salvation to all who believe what he has promised." There must be belief; otherwise, it would be magic. But notice the verbs: God *forgives, delivers,* and *gives*. Baptism perfectly pictures God's action. Remember when we said that in Lutheranism the teachings don't hang together like pearls on a string? They proceed from a glowing core, a warm and light center, which is the gospel of forgiveness. Baptism is a vivid way of knowing and having that core.

Luther explains how water can do such great things in a completely unsurprising way. It is not the water "but God's Word with the water and our trust in this Word." Water by itself is only water, but with the Word it gives life.

We have one more agenda item as we consider "what happens next?" What happens next if you have been baptized? Do you treasure a certificate? Is this something you are done with?

THE SACRAMENT OF HOLY BAPTISM

What is Baptism?
Baptism is not water only,
but it is water used together with God's
    Word and by his command.

What is this Word?
In Matthew 28 our Lord Jesus Christ says:
"Go therefore and make disciples of all nations,
baptizing them in the name of the Father
    and of the Son and of the Holy Spirit."

What benefits does God give in Baptism?
In Baptism God forgives sin,
delivers from death and the devil,
and gives everlasting salvation to all who
    believe what he has promised.

What is God's promise?
In Mark 16 our Lord Jesus Christ says:
"He who believes and is baptized
    will be saved;
but he who does not believe
    will be condemned."

How can water do such great things?
It is not water that does these things,
but God's Word with the water and our
    trust in this Word.
Water by itself is only water,
but with the Word of God
it is a life-giving water
which by grace gives the new birth
    through the Holy Spirit.

St. Paul writes in Titus 3:
"He saved us . . . in virtue of his own mercy,
by the washing of regeneration and
renewal in the Holy Spirit,
which he poured out upon us richly
through Jesus Christ our Savior,
so that we might be justified by his grace
and become heirs in hope of eternal life.
The saying is sure."

What does Baptism mean for daily living?
It means that our sinful self, with all its evil deeds and desires,
should be drowned through daily repentance;
and that day after day a new self should arise
to live with God in righteousness and purity forever.

St. Paul writes in Romans 6:
"We were buried therefore with him by Baptism into death,
so that as Christ was raised from the dead by the glory of the Father,
we too might walk in newness of life."

Not at all. The Catechism calls us to *daily* use of Baptism. Recall the picture of immersion. Paul writes in Romans 6: "We were buried therefore with him by Baptism into death, so that as Christ was raised from the dead by the glory of the Father, we too might walk in newness of life." The Catechism explains Paul's words: Baptism means that "our sinful self, with all its evil deeds and desires, should be drowned through daily repentance, and that day after day a new self should arise to live with God in righteousness and purity forever."

Now there is no point in envying the "born-again" churches. Lutheranism says you are born again and again and again. You are, and are to be, "born again" each day. If Lutherans often fail to live up to their faith, it is because of their guilt about yesterday and worry about tomorrow. There is no reason for guilt about yesterday. If a person repents and returns to Baptism, making an appeal to a forgiving God, there is no guilt. In a way, there is no yesterday, if by that we mean a reckoning sheet of wrongs. And there is no reason for worry about tomorrow. If a person repents and returns to Baptism, making an appeal to a providing God, there is no worry. In a way, there is no tomorrow, if by that we mean a need to prove ourselves right before God. We are free for today. We are new persons, new beings, beings who are "as Christ" or even, to the neighbor, "a Christ." God looks at us and sees the innocence of Christ, the first-born of the new creation in which we begin to take part. Baptism pictures this and gives it.

Let's consider more carefully the word *repent*. It is possible that we picture repentance as a gloomy activity of sour and somber, even self-hating people. But this is wrong. The New Testament pictures repentance as a painful act and a joyful act. We hate to let go of ourselves and our sin. This is the painful part. But when we do, the gospel tells us it is like putting on the best garments for a wedding, because Christ, the bridegroom, is here. This is the joy of repentance. It means shrugging off the old, letting go, and letting

God act. Then it means turning, so that where the old self had been, we are turned and the new self in Christ appears. We have heard the promise and we cling to it. Thus each day is new. Each day we are called. Each day we are nurtured.

Lutheran teaching says that repentance "is really nothing else than Baptism," with its "entering upon a new life." The Large Catechism says that "if you live in repentance, therefore, you are walking in Baptism, which not only announces this new life but also produces, begins, and promotes it." Baptism is not just a picture or a means, but it is a working out of grace.

And the Lord's Supper. Except where there is much population growth or many conversions, Lutherans will not have as many Baptisms as Lord's Suppers. More and more congregations observe the Lord's Supper, the Eucharist, at least once each Lord's day. Sunday is their holy day to celebrate the resurrection. And on that day they recall that the disciples knew the risen Lord "in the breaking of the bread." Scholars suggest that the early Christians would always observe this meal on the Lord's day in order to recognize Christ's presence in a special way. Not all Lutheran congregations have the sacrament each Sunday; they still observe it frequently, and revere this picture and means of grace, this way of announcing and realizing God's call and nurture.

The Lord's Supper, we remember, observes the simple meal of Jesus with his disciples the night he was betrayed, the night before he died. Luther once said we should try to make our supper as much like the original one as possible. He did not mean we had to study ancient archaeology and architecture and custom in order to reproduce the room and the style. He meant we should make possible the gift of grace that came with the meal.

Thus the Lord's Supper has us look backward to the story of Israel. Some gospel accounts see it as a Passover meal—a *seder* of the sort your Jewish friends observe in their homes each spring. It recalls how God "passed over" the doorposts of the Israelites in Egypt that had blood smudged on them. God then delivered Israel, while Egypt experienced death. But the Lord's Supper also has us look forward. Jesus says that he had longed to have this meal with the disciples—with us—and that he would have it again in his kingdom. It is a foretaste of the banquet to be held in the new age, in the new time. It is the "heavenly banquet." Jesus tells the disciples that he "earnestly desired" this meal—the quaint language of the gospel lets us know how important the Supper is to him (Luke 22:14-23).

And we respond, in repentance and in faith, by examining our hearts, joining a congregation, receiving the bread and the wine, receiving Christ. Libraries are full of books about debates over the meanings of this meal, and rivers of ink have been poured to complicate it. There are no winners and losers in these debates and there may not be simple villains or heroes. Lutherans have made their contribution to controversy. Today, happily, more and more Christians are converging. Lutherans and Roman Catholics, for instance,

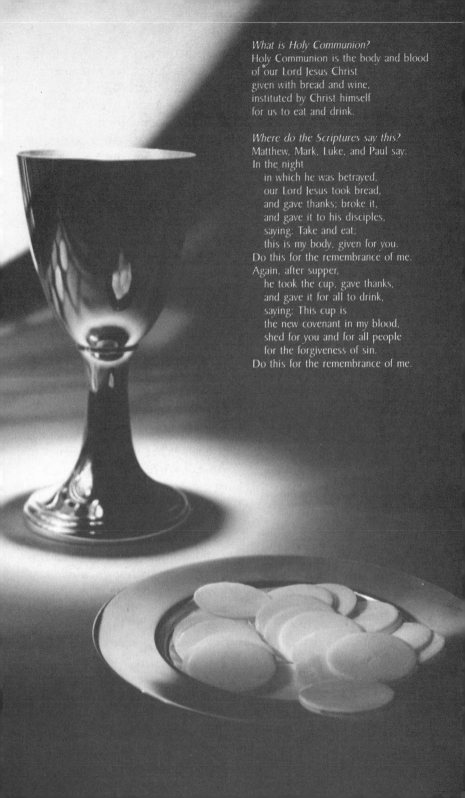

What is Holy Communion?
Holy Communion is the body and blood
of our Lord Jesus Christ
given with bread and wine,
instituted by Christ himself
for us to eat and drink.

Where do the Scriptures say this?
Matthew, Mark, Luke, and Paul say:
In the night
   in which he was betrayed,
   our Lord Jesus took bread,
   and gave thanks; broke it,
   and gave it to his disciples,
   saying: Take and eat;
   this is my body, given for you.
Do this for the remembrance of me.
Again, after supper,
   he took the cup, gave thanks,
   and gave it for all to drink,
   saying: This cup is
   the new covenant in my blood,
   shed for you and for all people
   for the forgiveness of sin.
Do this for the remembrance of me.

have agreed on the understanding of the presence of Christ in the meal, and may one day be enjoying each others' fellowship at the table that is the Lord's, not the Lutherans' or the Catholics'.

So we will not revisit the old controversies over the Lord's Supper except where the Lutheran understanding locates itself. On one hand, it refuses to see the Lord's Supper as only a picture or a symbol—as something we fill with meanings out of our own spiritual life. No, to remember a strange phrase in our first session: in the Lord's Supper something really happens. It does not *not* happen. On the other hand, Lutherans refuse to see the elements of the Lord's Supper in a magical way, as if bread and wine became physical objects that have all the same properties that Jesus' body and blood did, except that you cannot see the change. No, faith must be bonded with the bread and the wine through the Word if anything is to happen.

What benefits do we receive from this sacrament?
The benefits of this sacrament are pointed
out by the words,
given and shed for you for the remission
of sins.
These words assure us that in the sacrament
we receive forgiveness of sins, life, and
salvation.
For where there is forgiveness of sins,
there is also life and salvation.

How can eating and drinking do all this?
It is not eating and drinking that does this,
but the words, *given and shed for you
for the remission of sins.*
These words, along with eating and
drinking, are the main thing in the sacrament.
And whoever believes these words
has exactly what they say,
forgiveness of sins.

So we have a text that tells our Lutheran position: "Holy Communion is the body and blood of our Lord Jesus Christ given with bread and wine, instituted by Christ himself for us to eat and drink." The Catechism quotes three gospels and the apostle Paul to tell the story behind the meal. What are the benefits of this meal? We receive "forgiveness of sins, life, and salvation." Here is the old glowing core theme again. It always comes back to this point!

There is no magic. "It is not eating and drinking" that does all this good, but the words, *given and shed for you for the remission of sins.* These words, along with the eating and drinking, are "the main thing in the sacrament." This is something special. "And whoever believes these words has exactly what they say, forgiveness of sins." As you believe, so you have, says Luther about the gifts of the Word of God.

You may ask about how to prepare yourself for the Lord's Supper. You will treat it as special. Some people fast, to get themselves ready, but you do not have to. To be ready you only have to believe the words, "given and shed for you for the remission of sins." And then the astonishing thing occurs: the words "for you" get singled out. The whole gospel story, the memory of Israel and the hope of the heavenly banquet, the libraries of debates and rivers of ink, the hundreds of thousands of occurrences of this meal, this day—all these finally come down to the "for you." Something is not gospel unless it is "for you." The Lord's Supper is a marvelous way of picturing and then realizing this. *You* are the focus. *For you* Christ died. The Holy Spirit is calling *you*. It is *you* who repents, who responds in faith, who receives. No one can live your life for you—though Christ already has. You alone can be drowned with Jesus Christ, can receive this bread and wine at his table through your mouth, and you alone can grasp it in faith. You alone can live your new life. The Lord's Supper makes this clear, because of the Word connected with it.

When is a person rightly prepared to receive this sacrament?
Fasting and other outward preparations serve a good purpose.
However, that person is well prepared and worthy who believes these words.
given and shed for you for the remission of sins.
But anyone who does not believe these words, or doubts them,
is neither prepared nor worthy,
for the words *for you* require simply a believing heart.

The Large Catechism reminds us that "the custom has been retained by us of not administering the sacrament to those who have not previously been examined and absolved." Such examination and absolution can occur personally. You can take your plaguing sins directly to the pastoral confessor. This confessor has ways of hearing your burden and personalizing forgiveness. You also examine yourself as you participate with the whole congregation in the act of confession that precedes so many eucharists. But even more, your whole life is to be one of examining, confessing, repenting.

Do you get "good enough" by confessing to have a ticket to the Lord's Supper? That's not how it works. That would again be your achievement instead of God's perfect action. So the Large Catechism goes on to say: "If you are heavy-laden and feel your weakness, go joyfully to the sacrament and receive refreshment, comfort, and strength." So, says that Catechism, the Lord's Supper "is given as a *daily* food and sustenance so that our faith may refresh and strengthen itself and not weaken in the struggle but grow continually stronger;" it is "a great . . . treasure which is daily administered and distributed among Christians." This does not mean that

Christians must commune daily, but in repentance and response they "return" to the Lord's Supper, as they do to Baptism, daily.

SUMMARY AND REFLECTION

We have called these last sections "Summary and Reflection." In this last and seventh session, the reasons for this name ought to be most clear of all. Baptism and the Lord's Supper are themselves summaries of all that faith is. In them, God the command-giver commands that we do something. Yet the reason for divine command now becomes most clear: the demands occur for our good. In the sacraments, God the promise-giver extends the promise "for you."

The Christian faith is not a set of principles but a story, a story that pictures and gives the loving action of God in Christ to believers. Baptism and the Lord's Supper recall this story and, by the power of the Holy Spirit—they make this story our own. When we become part of the plot of this story, we learn that as we face a world of injustice and hatred, we are to judge it according to the law of God, and examine ourselves in light of that law. Then in the same plot, as we face this world we find that the grace which is most needed is grace that says "for you."

Reflection can mean something like an image in a mirror. Baptism and the Lord's Supper are mirrors held up to the whole divine action, and then imaged in our life. Up to now in our study, reflection has meant that we think about what has just been taught, we try to make it our own. It is the same now as we reflect about Baptism and the Lord's Supper. They are brief acts; they take minutes. Yet they inspire the reflection that we make them, and the story, and the God behind them, our own. And we should. The whole point about a faith that lets God be God is to see its focus: it is for you.

1. If someone asked you, "What is the gospel?" what would you say?

2. If someone asked you, "What attracts you about the Lutheran church?" what would you say?

3. Reflect on your response to the critical question for Session 1, Do I belong here? How would you address that question now, having completed the inquirer's class?

4. What questions remain for you at the end of this inquiry?